FROM

Mouths of Men

BLACK MEN SPEAK FREELY AND FRANKLY ABOUT BLACK WOMEN, RELATIONSHIPS, LOVE AND SEX

ALWIN PETER

INGLIS PUBLICATIONS

First published 1998 in Great Britain by Inglis Publications
PO Box 16819, London E13 9RP

ISBN 0 953 2477 0 8

This is a work of non-fiction

Typeset by Pek Media, London

Printed and bound in Great Britain by
Cox & Wyman, Reading, Berkshire

Dedicated to black women... past, present and future.
'You are owed a debt we have not even began to repay'.

ACKNOWLEDGEMENTS

All things in life are possible. This book has been more than 18 months in the making. During that time I have experienced all the emotions known to man (or woman) kind. I felt excited getting my first response through the post. I felt angry on opening the envelope only to find it empty. I felt frustrated when, after three months and having given out hundreds of questionnaires, only 30 were returned. I felt like giving up when I lost half the work I had spent hours analysing. I was mad as hell at many people who made promises they could not, or did not, keep.

I learned many lessons in undertaking this project. The most important being that you are not defeated until you admit defeat; you are not down and out until you refuse to rise up from adversity.

I would be doing a great injustice to many people if I accepted sole credit for this book. I am truly indebted to the black men who took part in this project. Special thanks to Frank and Victor who were the first ones to return the questionnaire and who encouraged several others to do the same. Special thanks to the black men I interviewed who were honest and forthright in their opinions.

I would like to acknowledge the help given to me by my brother Andre; my sister Anaethea, whose opinion I often sought and whose patience I am sure was stretched beyond endurance; my mum, in-laws and the rest of my family-the support was much appreciated. Special thanks to Aida-your views were the turning point. Rosemary, I truly thank you for your support, help and encouragement; more so when I was thinking about pressing the 'button'. Respect and heartfelt gratitude goes out to P I, my role model and would-be mentor. Judy, what can I say?

I would also like to express gratitude to Susan Delgardo, Peter Pek, J. Miller, D.O., Jason, Pauline, Howard and Martin for their professional help and guidance.

I am also indebted to many people who supported, offered advice and encouraged me throughout: Carolette, Linda and friends, work friends, training partners, and an army of friends-you know who you are. The models Ade, Del, Joseph, Lawrence, Raymond and Tony Richards Photography who all went beyond the call of duty, I thank you. Lastly, I would like to acknowledge the people who said it could not be done or that I could not do it. Your doubts and negativity kept me going. I proved you all wrong. I knew I would.

API 1998

INTRODUCTION

I recently ran into an old friend. After exchanging the usual greetings, she asked what I was doing. I said I was writing a book.

"A book huh. What is it about?"

"About relationships."

" Ok." She sighed as she gave me that 'oh-not-another-one' look.

" From what angle are you going to approach the book? Have you got anything new to say about the relationship between black men and women? Is there anything left to say?" she asked without once stopping for breath. She went on to tell me what she thought of black men.

" Men are dogs. Men are no good. You cannot trust a man. Women make more money than men. We are now independent, we do not need men..."

"Wait a minute," I snapped, interrupting her in mid-flow. "I believe I have heard this before. If, as many people have said, there is a problem with black men and women forming relationships, then that problem cannot be solved by regurgitating stereotypical views. What about women? Do you think black women have contributed to the current state of affairs? Or do you think the problem lies only with black men?" I confidently asked.

She looked me up and down, sucked her teeth and continued her attack. You may recognise some of her statements; you may even have uttered them at some stage.

"...all the good black men are married, engaged, married to white women or gay. A good man is so hard to find. Black men will run the other way if you act like you really love them and want to marry them. Marriage is like a prison sentence to black men; they fear more successful women..."

As she rambled on, it struck me that a great number of the books written about relationships are written by women, for women. The voices of black men are often silent. Their views unknown, overlooked, assumed, generalised or totally ignored, thus giving rise to myths, mistrust, misunderstanding, hurt, half-truths and damn lies. It was at this stage that I decided to devote the book to the views of black men, in particular their views on black women, relationships, love and sex.

This book is different from other books. It contains the most popular answers to questions that were asked to black men who have dated, or are dating black women. The questions and answers formed the basis of the three main chapters of the book. I selected the questions on the basis of the interviews I did with black women, asking them what questions they would like black men to answer. I also did the same with black men, getting their views and opinions on the sorts of questions they would like asked.

More than 350 black men were either interviewed or answered my questionnaire. I cannot in all honesty say the selection method was scientifically based. I gave the questionnaire out at various events inviting black men to return it in a prepaid envelope. The men I interviewed ranged in age from 18 to 61; their occupations were just as varied, ranging from university students, to the unemployed, to lawyers. As we are not all alike, the men interviewed were British born, some were African born others were of West Indian origin. What follows is the truth as told from the MOUTHS OF BLACK MEN.

PART ONE

Brothers on women

" ...Some black women are becoming the men they wanted to marry. Black women own their own homes, are employed, are earning good salaries and are independent, often without kids."

"... Women should not expect men to be more like women."

**"I don't know what it is with women, but they get mixed up when it comes
to sex. Sex is sex, love is love. No connection between the two..."**

"There are only two things I dislike about today's black women – I dislike all they say and all they do. Apart from that, I have no problem with black women..."

After showing the rough draft of this chapter to my female friends, some of them felt the views expressed by men on women were harsh, unjustifiably hostile and negative towards black women. This took me by surprise. It was never my intention to produce a book that was negative towards black women.

On a number of occasions I was tempted to alter this chapter. I decided against it because it would have meant the book was not a true reflection of the views expressed to me by black men. Further, to alter what was written and said would be to destroy the very essence of the book. The book would not then be from the mouths of black men, but rather from the mouth of the author.

Black male-bashing has become fashionable in the last few years. Hardly a day goes by without someone telling us what they think of black men. Black men have been portrayed as an endangered species, brutes who are not capable of sustaining a relationship, men who are not responsible. They are women abusers and users, lay-abouts, drug users, abusers and sellers. The list could go on and on.

Now the tables are turned; it is time for black men to state their views. The opinions black men have of black women, I am glad to say, are not as negative, but they do speak the truth as they see it. My guess is that many people will be uncomfortable with a lot of what black men have said in this chapter. I know at times the views expressed by my fellow black men disturbed me. For instance, one of the black men I interviewed said he saw dark-skinned women as being primitive and sexual, whereas he saw light-skinned women as potential partners. I do know we as black people play the skin colour game, but to have such outrageous and demented views shows that some of us are still slaves, if not physically then most definitely mentally.

Whether or not you agree with all that is said, one fact is undeniable: black men have spoken to black women and about black women. In this chapter men state what they dislike about black women, what they love about black women, and the questions they would like to ask black women. The views offered are wide-ranging, often taking into account the changing role of women within society and the failures of black men towards black women.

1 What do you dislike about black women?

IF white people were to say all black people were the same and that you cannot trust black people, we would rightly say they were racist, ignorant, stupid and, as such, dismiss them as we know the statement to be false. My question to black women is this, 'What do you say to people who think all black men are the same and that you cannot trust a black man. Are they right? Are they sexist? Are they ignorant? Is it possible that all black men are not the same'?

Judging from the response to the question, it appears that the number one dislike of black men is the fact that black women tend to pre-judge and assume the worst. Some 40 per cent of men mentioned this as a major dislike with 15 per cent saying that black women are not very approachable.

Numbers in brackets represent the percentage of the sample.

Black women who pre-judge and assume the worst about black men (40 per cent)

It is pointless trying to tell black women you are not how they think you are. It is all the more difficult if the woman in question had a bad experience with a black man. Black women have a habit of punishing black men in general for the crimes of individual black men. By all means condemn the behaviour, but do not condemn the black male species. I have never done any scientific research, nonetheless I have found in my relationships with black women over the years the following to be typical of their views:
(1) Men are dogs. I have heard this one literally a million or more times.
(2) We are womanisers.
(3) We like light-skinned women. I can't even remember the number of times I have heard dark-skinned women complain about being ignored by black men in preference to light-skinned women.
(4) One of my favourites: men only think of one thing, sex.
(5) Black men dislike commitment/responsibility.
(6) We are sexist.
(7) We make poor fathers. The deeds of a few affecting the majority.
(8) We only think of ourselves.
(9) All good black men are gay or married. (This one, I believe, gets better with time for black women. A black single woman is not happy unless she utters this one at least twice a month.)
(10) Never trust a black man.

I apologise profusely to black women if I missed out your favourite put-down of the black man. Please understand that my response was limited to the space provided in the questionnaire. **Anonymous**

Tell me honestly, have you ever met a black woman who did not have an opinion about black men? You have a greater chance of being struck twice by lightning. In the same spot than finding a black woman who does not have a negative opinion of black men. Black women have made up their minds that we are untrustworthy. We do not take responsibility for our actions and we like white women despite the fact that the majority of black men choose to be with black women.

I love black women. I have never been out with the enemy. I believe I am trustworthy and I am definitely responsible, still you get sisters coming with the negative vibes. As a community, the only discrimination we find acceptable and actively encourage, is the continued discrimination against black men by black women. Black women are not truly happy unless they can tell you how low black men are.

I dislike immensely women who pre-judge black men unfairly. If black women do not change their attitude towards black men I believe the percentage of black men going out with and marrying white women is going to rise. **Kimbro**

They say that there are only two things certain in life, death and taxes. Well I would like to add a third. I guarantee you that black women will have a negative stereotypical opinion of black men. The sad thing is that often that negativity is based on hearsay, myth, lies and general bullshit. **Anonymous**

Ladies, be honest. How many times have you said, 'I trust no black man?'. Women may not be happy with certain black men who have let them down in the past. This, however, does not and should not give them the right to condemn all black men. If I had to give black women any advice it would be not to paint all of us with the same brush. Assuming the worst of anyone usually brings out the worst in them. Not all men are dogs. If we are all dogs, then women are bitches for wanting dogs. Get rid of the negativity. It serves no one. We are stronger together than apart. **Rayon**

Women who are high-maintenance/materialistic (20 per cent)

After the breakup of a very long relationship, my friends fixed me a blind date. It took me by surprise that this woman expected me to pay for the entire evening without even the pretence of volunteering to contribute at all. I seriously doubt that she had brought any money with her. I did not expect her to pay. If she had offered to pay I would have refused. But the fact she automatically expected me to pay bothered me. She was most definitely a high-maintenance woman, the type of woman who always expects you to pick up the tab, irrespective of her financial situation. I dislike black women who are high-maintenance.

The least women could do is offer to make a contribution. If it is a new partner, nine out of ten times the man would object and insist on paying anyway. A woman can create a good impression by insisting on at least making a contribution or suggesting that she pays on a subsequent date. If you enjoyed each other's company you are more likely to invite her out again if she at least offered a contribution towards the bill. **William**

As a black man with an average salary, I hate black women who are high-maintenance. By high- maintenance I mean women who have very expensive taste and who expect that taste to be met by men. High maintenance women seldom pay on dates and rarely part with their money, if they have any. **Anonymous**

A small percentage of today's black women are too materialistic. The only thing on their minds is getting the best clothes, the latest designer wear, and a flash car. I will say in their defence that black people on the whole are extremely materialistic. We must always have the latest in fashion, music, cars, and whatever designer label is the phattest, darkest, dope and roughest.The problem with this attitude is that we teach our children–girls included–to be materialistic.

So, to be fair materialistic women are taught to be that way from a young age. Adults plant the seed by always giving young boys and girls the latest fashions and the most expensive gifts. We should not be surprised if a few women grow up expecting the same things. If they cannot provide it themselves, they expect men to provide it. I hate materialistic black women all the same. **Anonymous**

I hate black women who are materialistic. Materialistic women will be the first ones to complain about decent men. What they mean is not that they cannot find a decent man; more like they cannot find a rich enough one to give them all the things they want.

Materialistic women cannot provide the nice things in life for themselves because more often than not they are failures in life and career. Materialistic women judge a man by the size of his wallet and not by his character. I have dated some of these women; they are empty vessels. The only good thing is that they are a small minority. The majority of black women are not that way. **Anonymous**

Black women are not very approachable (15 per cent)

I can sum up what I hate about today's black women in one word- **unapproachability.** My opinion on today's black women is that they are not the most approachable. Too many black women have an attitude that says, 'do not approach just keep walking.' It takes a strong man to approach a black woman.

I have spoken to a number of black women who agree they are not the most approachable of women. One woman I spoke to went as far as saying she feels sorry for black men as she too acknowledged that black women are not very approachable. **Anonymous**

Why do you think so many black men are rejecting black women? It is because they are so dam unapproachable. This is one of the things that really pisses me off about black women. I work in an environment where I come into contact with a lot of women. I have found more often than not, that white women are more open and friendly when you approach them. Black women are often hostile, closed, and very suspicious. They think you have an ulterior motive. Their guards are always up, they are too quick to give a black man a hard time. I have never dated a white woman and never will but I cannot in all honesty say black women are very approachable. Often the good guys are reluctant to approach black women, therefore the bad 'bwoys' are the ones who end up with them. **Gary**

Today's black women are not always the most approachable; they can be intimidating and a turn-off. I have dated women from different cultures. It hurts me to say it, but black women are the least welcoming. They are too much hard work, they have too much attitude. If you have ever been to a night club you will understand what I mean. There are literally hundreds of single black women, but the majority of them are so cold-looking you would not ask them to dance, much less for a date. Maybe they have reason to be so distant-I don't know. A little more openness would not hurt them if they want a partner. **Jason**

It is amazing how many of today's black women are so unapproachable, yet they will tell you differently. Whether they want to believe it or not, at times they come across as unapproachable. This is the honest truth from a black man who has never dated a woman from a different race. **Anonymous**

Women who deny their blackness and are multi-cultural (10 per cent)

Women who deny their blackness get on my nerves. For whatever reason, certain black women choose to deny their blackness. These types of women are easy to spot; they are usually the only black person in a pub. More often than not they have white partners and do all they can to avoid meeting other black people. **Bradley**

We as black people are messed up. Black women are no exception. According to the media all black people are worthless, unemployed, unambitious, and are all living in the 'ghetto,' taking drugs. The problem is that some black people buy into that image. If black women do not fit into that stereotypical image created by white people, they think they are special. They cannot possibly be black. As a result they adopt white culture. Increasingly, black successful women are falling into this trap. The truth of the matter is that for every person that fits the stereotype, there are thousands who do not. I therefore hate, successful black women (and men) who deny their culture.

Asian people and other minority groups who are far more successful do not, on the whole, deny their roots and they earn hundreds of millions a year. So why black people who earn £20,000 upwards a year feel the need to disown their people is beyond comprehension. **Anonymous**

I hate black women who refuse to see colour. In Jungle Fever, the Spike Lee movie, one of the women refers to 'rainbow-fucking women'. These women go out with any breed of man; name the race and she has been there and done it. They remind me of Captain Kirk of **Star Trek** fame; he went with anything, from green aliens to women with four eyes.

Multi-cultural black women are lost; they often expect you to be like the men they have dated, often comparing you to Asian, Jewish, white European, and Arabic men. In a racist society they choose to ignore colour, thus dealing with prejudice by going with men of any colour. The truth of the matter is that colour does matter. I know of black women who are going out with men from different ethnic backgrounds where the man's parents do not know he is dating a black woman. Rainbow-fucking women choose to turn a blind eye to any thing pertaining to race. They give in before the fight against racism has been won. **Anonymous**

Weaves that are too long /too much make-up/ blue contact lenses/blonde hair (7 per cent)

I must admit I do not care for black women who wear **too** much make up. I swear to god, I went out with a woman who wore so much make-up that when we were dancing she left her face print on my designer shirt. **Rupert**

I once met this woman at a party. She had a dope body. I really did not pay much attention to her face; anyway we ended up in bed. The following morning I thought her grandmother had brought me breakfast in bed until I realised it was the same woman without make-up. From that day I became very weary of black women who wear too much make-up. **Anonymous**

I met what I thought was a fine light-skinned woman at a wine bar recently. After a few drinks she came back to my place. She got undressed. I could not believe it. The woman's body was so dark, much darker in comparison to her neck and face. I did not know whether to laugh or cry seeing this woman who resembled a black and white minstrel. Her face had so much foundation it was amazing. **Phil**

Nothing gets to me as much as when I see black women with blond hair and blue contact lenses. You people look fucking stupid. Take it off. Black women who have blonde wigs, blue or other coloured contact lenses and weaves all the way to their asses have psychological problems. I believe they have bought into the European idea of beauty.

Black women were not born with blue eyes or blonde hair. Why do they feel it necessary to take on the characteristics of white people? Undoubtedly, they will tell you it is only fashion. How can you destroy your identity for fashion?

I wonder what white people think when they see Negro women with blue eyes and blond hair. They must be laughing. **Emmanuel**

I dislike black women who wear weaves the length of their back. It does not make sense; everyone knows it is false. The majority of men I have spoken to are not against weaves as such. What they really, really hate are black women who have the weave so long that it becomes obvious it is a weave. **Anonymous**

Women who use black men as excuses (5 per cent)

I hate women who use men as excuses for the failures in their own life. I asked a black woman who I met recently what type of black man is she interested in meeting. She said she is interested in a man who is not threatened by the fact she is earning more, is in a better job and generally has better prospects in life than him. This woman who has a well-paid job but who by no means has a substantial income is already making assumptions about black men. In her mind she has the perfect excuse for not having a black man. Her excuse is that "black men are threatened by my success and therefore cannot deal with successful black women." She assumes, prior to meeting a black man, that she is going to be better, richer and an all round better individual.

From my point of view, women like her are suffering from an illness. Some women get this illness from reading too many books, magazines and newspaper articles and watching too many films. The result is that these women get the bug that tells them they are now all super women, with super jobs and super earning power. They can now dump on black men, who are by all accounts penniless, powerless and jobless. The truth is that most of those women are one paycheck away from poverty. **AI**

I hate black women who use black men as excuses for dating white men. If they choose to be with white men, so be it. But those fake wannabe sisters who tell you they are with white men because... Because black men are not romantic. Because black men are brutes. Because black men have not got money. Because black men are bad. Because black men are emotionally retarded. Because black men are not as successful. Because, because, because.

Stop using black men as excuses for the choices you make in life. You go out with white men not because of black men, but because you want to. It is amazing how these women run to one white man after another. **Anonymous**

The only thing I dislike about black women (and this does not extend to all black women) is the mentality that all black men are 'no good' and that men of other races are much better. What I do not think they realise is that women of other races make similar complaints of their own men. This means that instead of admitting going out with a man of a different race because they want to they use black men as an excuse. **Anonymous**

Women who are too giving of themselves (3 per cent)

Black women can be so strong in term of career, getting educationally qualified and in surviving generally. Nonetheless, they can be so weak in relationships. I dislike the fact that some black women deny themselves happiness and the freedom to be themselves because they have committed themselves to a blind loyalty in a relationship, a relationship that is often not productive or worth keeping. **Anonymous**

I do not understand some black women. Some black women are too giving. This is one of the main differences between men and women, not just black women but women generally. They are too eager to please a man in a relationship. If the relationship is bad men are more likely than women to walk away. Why women think they have to stay loyal to a worthless man and a futile relationship is beyond me.

I hate black women who are too giving to the wrong men. If these types of men are allowed to get away with their behaviour who should we blame? Women (like my mum) who allow my dad to get away with all sorts of shit? Or should we blame men for taking advantage?

A well-known feminist once said 'If a man abuses you physically or mentally, the first time it happens it is the man to blame. The second, tenth, hundredth time it happens then it is your (the woman's) fault for staying and allowing yourself to become a victim.' Her point, which I agreed with, is that you have a choice. You don't have to stay in a relationship that is abusive or one sided. **TPI**

2 What makes you feel uncomfortable about a black woman?

IT was very difficult to get the men I interviewed to open up and say exactly what made them feel uncomfortable about being with black women. The reason often given was 'It shows our weakness and venerability and in some cases our failures.' For men to admit to what makes them feel uncomfortable is to admit to the fact that they do not have the same ability as their partner or they cannot operate at the same level. In what is perceived as a male-dominated society, some men feel threatened by a more powerful, assertive and independent female partner.

Independent (25 per cent)

Black women are becoming more independent. They are taking up educational and job opportunities and I think they have made a forward step in asserting themselves in the world. Some black men feel uncomfortable with the emerging independence of black women. If they are independent what do they need us (black men) for. We do not want to be independent of our women, so why do they feel the need to be independent of us? **Anonymous**

Today's black women are independent to a degree they have not been before. It is new to them and to a great number of black men. As a result the male community is having to adjust. Some men meet the challenge, some are threatened by it and thus do not know how to react. Others turn to violence as a means of controlling these women or turn to women from other races. Irrespective of how we as black men choose to react to the increasing independence of black women, we have no one but ourselves to blame. If black men do not take the lead then our women will. **Anonymous**

It is good that black women are becoming more independent. However, the majority of black men are uncomfortable with the term 'independent black women'. Often independent means independent of black men. That, to my mind, is a sad state of affairs and should not be celebrated. What other race can you think of where the women are proud of being independent of their men.

The independence of black women is a shame. A shame on black men as it shows the failure of black men to take responsibility. I am not a sexist, I believe in equality. My girlfriend has a very highly paid job. She is independent in that she can provide for herself financially. That is to be applauded and encouraged. We are equal and need each other, we do not see ourselves being independent of each other. Many of my girlfriend's female friends see themselves as being independent of men not only financially but emotionally . The idea of finding a black man has become alien to them. Wherever the problem lies, black women should not feel the need to be independent in that way. **Berry**

Does it matter at all if black women are more independent? Black women are undoubtedly more independent. They are more independent of their men. More independent to pay their way in life. More independent to move away from the traditional role of women within society. It is good that black women are more independent. However, what will the implication be for black men? I cannot think of a single black man who can honestly say they are comfortable with independent black women.

Although my answer should be restricted to my views of black women today, I cannot help but mention that the independence of black women should be a signal to black men to get their shit together and focus on the things that are important in life. I know it is difficult being a black man in a white dominated society, but we cannot give up the fight for economic parity with all manner of man and woman. **Anonymous**

Women who are more sexually experienced (23 per cent)

It is great to have a more sexually experienced woman. The drawback is that you keep thinking of how she got that experience. You imagine her with all sorts of men, doing all sorts of things. You feel inadequate in that she is the one leading and showing you all sorts of new things. In most cases you have never thought of doing such things. You worry also about what she may be thinking about you. All sorts of thoughts pop into your head. Maybe she thinks I am a virgin. She probably thinks I have only had sex in the missionary position. Maybe she is comparing me to other men. I am sure I am not as good as her last lover. You worry so much now you cannot perform. You cannot get lift-off. Mission control has grounded you. **Paul**

I feel uncomfortable if a woman is more sexually experienced because it makes me feel inadequate. Men are the ones who should know more in bed. My woman should not be telling me what to do and how. A woman who has too much sexual experience cannot be any good. I believe she must be a loose woman. These types of women make me very uncomfortable. **Anonymous**

I love sex, I want it 24:7 and usually get it too. For a woman to be more sexually experienced than me would be a novelty and I would welcome the opportunity to test her sexual know-how. In the long run I could never have a serious relationship with a woman who is more experienced than me. **Anonymous**

Women who are too possessive/dependent (15 per cent)

I cannot think of anything that makes a man more uncomfortable than a possessive woman. She is like a boomerang; irrespective of how much you throw her away she always comes back to you. **AK**

A possessive woman is like a racist with a gun at the carnival-dangerous. Possessive women are like your second skin; they are always there. They call you every day, want to be be with you everyday, never leave you alone. That is why I feel extremely uncomfortable with possessive women. **Adrian**

Women who earn more (15 per cent)

Women should not earn more than men. It is not right. That definitely makes me feel uncomfortable. **Leo**

I used to feel uncomfortable with women who earned more than me. Recently I have come to realise that what matters is not so much the woman earning more but rather how she treats her partner. Also, what the partner is doing for himself. If you really love your partner it should not matter who earns more. Society says men should be the breadwinner. I believe this is sexist nonsense. Once I have enough money to take care of myself, contribute to the household bills, buy whatever I want within reason and put money away for the mortgage, it does not bother me who earns more. **Anonymous**

If she is very financially established and I am not, that would make me feel uncomfortable. She may be very critical even if you are doing your best. **Anonymous**

If my partner is earning more than me it is not really a problem unless she rubs it in my face. If she makes me feel small or inadequate or shows me up in public, then that makes me feel uncomfortable. **Jeff**

In a society dominated by machoism it makes me feel uncomfortable when women who I am dating earn more than me. If most men are honest with themselves, they will agree with me. **Alexander**

Women who demand commitment too soon (10 per cent)

I have been out with women where after two or three dates expected me to make a commitment to them. Women who expect you to make a commitment too quickly make me feel uncomfortable. Men usually take their time in making up their minds. If a man decides against a relationship the woman usually gets angry and says all men are the same. Women often jump to the wrong conclusion, they presume the man is interested in forming a long-term relationship when in fact he is still making up his mind. **Stephen**

I sometimes feel that after sleeping with a woman she automatically assumes that you want a relationship or you are going to marry her. That makes me feel uncomfortable. **MS**

Women who bring too much baggage into a relationship (4 per cent)

Human beings do not live in a vacuum. We interact with each other, and because of this we develop hang-ups, rules, regulations, in short, we develop baggage. In my limited experience women tend to cling on to excess baggage, more so in relation to men. I feel extremely uncomfortable when a woman brings all the excess baggage from an old relationship into a new one. My ex-girlfriend had not gotten over her relationship with her old boyfriend. It proved impossible to develop a meaningful relationship with her, so we broke up. **Martin**

Women who always want to talk (3 per cent)

You have just made love to your partner. You feel good. All that remains is for you to sleep. You can't. Why. Because she wants to talk. Women tend to like to talk. Men do not always like to talk particularly about their feelings. This is a fact many women do not appreciate. I feel uncomfortable with women who always talk or who want me to talk. Anyway, why women want to talk after making love is a mystery that baffles me. **Geoffrey**

Women who are always late (2 per cent)

Who is usually late, men or women? My girlfriend says it's men. I don't think so, I believe it is women.

I have made a note of all the best excuses the women I have dated have used when they are late:

- The hairdresser was full. I missed my appointment.
- I could not get my hair done on time, put my make-up on in time find the right shoes to go with the dress.
- You want me to look good don't you? Well it takes time. I don't get up looking like this.
- My friend called and I could not get rid of her. You understand don't you?
- You have heard of black man's time. Well I was running on black woman's time. You have a problem with that? **MJ**

Women who are dishonest (2 per cent)

Dishonest women are dangerous. They lie about everything. You can never be quite sure if you should trust them. Broken heart, broken dreams, that is all you can expect from a dishonest woman. **Tee**

Women that are more intelligent (1 per cent)

Some men cannot cope with a woman more intelligent than them. It makes then feel inadequate and uncomfortable. Other men do not mind. It is really as simple as that. You cannot generalise. Different strokes for different folks. **Terry**

3 What do you find attractive/love about black women?

AS I mentioned earlier, over 350 black men took part in this study. When asked what they found attractive about black women, a great number of black men mentioned skin texture. However, I did not find a particular bias towards any particular shade. What I discovered, which I believe the majority of black people already know-is that we are still hung up about skin texture. Some black men prefer light-skinned women, others prefer brown-skinned women. Some prefer dark-skinned women, others prefer mixed-race partners.

To those who prefer a particular shade of black woman or man I advise you to read the words of Willie Lynch below.

Skin texture (30 per cent)

What I find really attractive about black women is the diversity in skin colour. You have the brown skinned-sister, to the darkest-skinned sisters to the light-skinned sisters. My favourite is the dark-skin sister; black coffee, no milk. **Anonymous**

When it comes to black women, you can have your coffee black, a little brown, or light-not-quite white. I am attracted to the light-skinned, not quite-white. **Anonymous**

Its funny-and I know a lot of women will not believe me since they have been systematically brainwashed into thinking black men prefer light-skinned women. The plain and simple fact is that I love dark-skinned women. Nothing turns me on more than making love to a dark skinned-sister. **Peter**

I find it ironic: the thing I love about black women repulses me. I love the fact that black women come in all shades, but to play the colour game is to do what white people expect. It is a divide and conquer technique whereby you divide the race by putting one skin texture against another. A strategy advocated by Willie Lynch, a British slave owner in the West Indies.

In a speech Willie Lynch gave to slave owners in Virginia in 1712, he said, "...I have a fool-proof method for controlling black slaves. I guarantee every one of you that if installed correctly, it will control the slaves for at least 300 years. My method is simple and members of your family and any Overseer can use it.

I have outlined a number of differences among the slaves; and I take these differences and make them bigger....Take this simple little list of differences and think about them. On top of my list is age, it is there only because it begins with A. The second is colour or shade. There is intelligence, size, sex, coarse hair or fine hair, tall or short, valley or hill, north, south, east or west. Now that you have a list of differences, I shall give you an outline of action. But before that, I shall assure you that distrust is stronger than trust and envy is stronger than adulation, respect and admiration.

The black slave, after receiving this indoctrination, shall carry on and will become self-refuelling and self-generating for hundreds of years, maybe thousands.

Don't forget you must pitch the old black versus the young black and the young black male against the old black male. **You must use the dark-skinned slave vs. the light-skinned slave and the light-skinned slave vs. the black-skinned slave.** You must also have your white servants and overseers distrust all blacks, but it is necessary that your slaves trust and depend on us. They must love , respect and trust only us.

Have your wife and children use them, never miss an opportunity...**The good thing about this plan is that if used for one year the slaves themselves will remain perpetually distrustful."**

Every time a black brother or sister plays the colour game, the Willie Lynch mind controlling and divisiveness technique succeeds in keeping us apart. Just love black women irrespective of their skin tone. We are proud people; we are no longer slaves. **Anonymous**

Call me what you like. One of the things I like about black women is the fact they come in shades. I love my light-skinned woman. This may be too controversial and therefore you may omit it from your book. Anyway, I love light skinned women. When you see a dark-skinned woman, you think primitive. You think animal sex, roughness. With a light-skinned woman, you think love. With a light-skinned woman you think marriage. You see niceness. You want her on your arm. I do not get the same feeling when I see a dark- skinned woman. **Anonymous**

They are black (25 per cent)

There is a popular saying that goes, 'it's a black thing you would not understand'. In relation to why I love black women it is as simple as that. I love them because they are black. It would never cross my mind to love any other woman. I understand this may be hard for some people to believe, but then again they would not understand. They are too busy loving white men and women. Or too busy trying to convince themselves colour does not matter. Or too busy trying to convince themselves they love black women while at the same time going out with women of any colour. **YG**

I love their natural black beauty. **SK**

I love black women because there is a history of love between black men and women. We share a common culture and there is a common bond. A bond you will never find with a woman from another race. This is a fact an increasing number of black men seem to have forgotten. **Anonymous**

I love black women because they are black. I can give you a 1000 reasons why I love them. However, not one of those reasons cannot be applied to women of any other race you care to choose. Further, if all the factors that I like in black women were present in any other woman I still would not consider them as a partner. The one deciding factor for me is race. There is nothing as special as a black woman. They are owed a debt that black men have not even begun to repay. **Anonymous**

Black women are achievers (20 per cent)

If there is one thing that sections of the black male community can learn from today's black women for certain, it is their desire to achieve. Black women can have it easier in a white society than black men who are always viewed as a threat. Black women at least prepare themselves to achieve in a white society, either by learning to compromise or at the very least by getting educationally qualified. Black women are among the largest groups of people returning to higher education. On one level, returning to higher education signifies a failure in earlier life; on the other hand, it also shows a determination to make up for past failures. **Anonymous**

I love the fact black women are achievers. Despite all the odds being stacked against them they still rise above adversity and achieve.

Black men do not often go on and achieve in later life. If you destroy the boy more often than not you have destroyed the man. **Charles**

I would like to congratulate black women for what they have achieved, but there is still a long way to go to make there presence not only felt but reckoned with. **Anonymous**

Looks/physical attraction (15 per cent)

It is difficult to narrow down what I like about black women as I like so much about them. However, if I was pushed then I would have to say I find their bodies extremely attractive. **DV**

The way a black woman looks will often determine whether I find her attractive. It is not the most important, but certainly one of the important things men notice. First impressions count. If you do not like the way someone looks, you will not take the time to get to know them. Therefore you will never know whether your impression of them was correct or not. The way you look will send out a message to a potential partner or a stranger. Make sure the message you send out by the way you look is the one you want people to have of you. Often black men love decently dressed women. **Rufus**

I will admit this is somewhat superficial, but what I find attractive about black women is that they have the biggest, most beautiful, sweetest looking asses on the planet. I am a sucker for a big ass. **Anonymous**

When it comes to what I love or find attractive about black women, without question it is the way they look. I guess like a lot of men I find that I love good-looking women. I like a trophy woman, so men can watch and gaze at her at parties, on the street and in clubs. **Philip**

As a black man I think black women are the sexiest around. They have rhythm-the way they move. I have been on this planet for more years than I care to remember and still I find black women have a sexiness that I have not seen in any other race. **Kenneth**

They are strong and are the soul, heart and protectors of the community (8 per cent)

Without doubt black women have held the black community together. This, my friend, is not empty rhetoric. How many of us have been brought up by black women? When men are missing who else is there? When men have faltered and have lost there way who was and is there still? The relationship between black men and black women is not perfect; we still have problem to sort out. Black women are not perfect, but I love them anyway. **Anonymous**

On the whole black women have remained true to their culture, and for that reason I will always love them. **Paul**

History makes me love black women. Throughout history they have been put upon, beaten, raped, enslaved, separated from their men, and still they rise. I love that fighting spirit. **Vincent**

Please, I beg you. Analyse the areas in which we say black women are strong-being single parents, coping with working and bringing up children, being single, being without men, surviving against the odds etc. etc., etc. I admire black women for their strength. Certain brothers must realise the strength of black women is a reflection of the weakness of black men. The weakness of black men in taking up their responsibilities and sharing the burden with black women. When talking about the legendary strength of black women we must be careful not to stereotype them. Also, we must not use the strength of black women as an excuse to dump on them. Still, enough respect to black women for being survivors. **Anonymous**

The majority of black women are strong. I love the fact that they are strong, but they are only strong because black men have been weak in certain areas. **Peter**

Ability to Dance (1 per cent)

I love many things about black women: their intelligence, tenderness, strength and compassion. I also love the way they dance. No woman on planet earth dances like black women. The expressiveness, the sexuality, the connection to our roots, the flexibility, the freedom, the energy, the joy the pain and the hope. All that and more I see when I watch sisters dance. **AL**

I love the way black women dance. If you have ever being to a soca fete and watched how the people let go; or an all black club when a popular song is played and everyone is dancing; or a party in the small hours of the night when the moon is about to disappear and the slow jam is about to start; then you will understand why I and a lot of other black men love the way black women dance. **Owen**

We love the Spirituality of black women (1%)

I love black women because they are the easiest women to love. As a black man who has finally found God I see a spirituality in black women that makes it easy for me to be attracted to them thus love them. You will be surprised how a woman is transformed once she believes in God. She glows with radiance. I really find that appealing in a black woman. **Anonymous**

I find spiritual women attractive. Spiritual in the widest sense, not necessarily religious. I love women who have found inner peace, women like Susan L Taylor and Iyanla Vanzant. These women constantly improve themselves through personal development. They are not dependent on anyone, they seek out new experiences, as a result they grow in inner strength and gain inner peace. These are the black women I find attractive. **Mark**

Strength of personality. They have a strong belief in themselves and powerful physiques. **Anonymous**

Their intelligence, their ability to articulate themselves. **Anonymous**

I love their tenderness, they can be very affectionate and are undoubtedly the most beautiful women on this planet. **Anonymous**

4 If you had the opportunity to ask black women any question, what would it be, and why?

THE questions black men want to ask black women may prove to be controversial. However, the right to ask these questions should not be denied. After all it is not often that black men are given the opportunity to speak freely and openly.

Do you know birth control exists? If you do, why do you not make more use of it?

Why is it that black women do not consider abortion like women of other races. If the man is not going to take care of his child, why on earth have the fucking baby. Birth control is way too advanced for our community to have so many young single parents. What's up with black women and birth control? **Anonymous**

I believe some black women use the withdrawal method. They allow the black man to come, then allow him to withdraw and disappear quick time. Leaving them pregnant and alone. You may not like my question, but please consider it before you dismiss it. Why is it that black women do not use the pill or some other form of birth control? As we approach the 21st century, our community should not have such a high level of lone black female-headed households. If black women say no, they are not having any children until they are married, then black men will marry them quick time. What is stopping them saying that to black men? **Anonymous**

I think birth control was only designed for white women. Somehow the pill does not appear to work for our young black women. Seriously though, I think I would have liked to ask the young women in the 1980s (when every other young girl was pushing a pram) why they did not use birth control. I am in principle against abortion, but I am tired of seeing children having children. **Jonathan**

What is it about abortion? Why is it that black women choose not to have an abortion? Why is it that parents are so happy for their young daughters to have children? Why do you not consider abortion? Do you like ruining your life before you have had a chance to live? **David**

How does it feel to be a black woman?

I believe today's women are at a crossroads. Their roles are, in a sense, becoming redefined. Some black women are becoming the men they wanted to marry. Black women own their own homes, are employed, earning good salaries, and are independent, often without kids. **Martin**

It must be difficult being a black woman in the 1990s. In the next few years black women will have to make very difficult decisions. For instance, should they do like black men and date outside their race? Should they go ahead and forge ahead of black men? Should they have to settle for and marry black men who may be less successful than them? Should they settle for a single life indefinitely? What about the divide between black women themselves? Not all black women are going to have successful jobs. A few of my successful women friends have said that they sometimes feel under attack from other black women because they do not depend on black men, are not on the dole or settling for less and most definitely have not got any kids and do not want any outside a caring relationship. **Toffi**

If you have a boy child whose father has deserted you, why do you take it out on the innocent child? Why do you not teach the boys to be different from their absent fathers?

I believe it took me 17, maybe 20, years before I came to terms with my mother. We are now on speaking terms. It took me a long time to get over the way she blamed me for my Dad not being with her. Single parents should understand the fact that they are single parents because they made the wrong choice in selecting a man. My mother and other mothers must realise I and other children are not, and should not be, held responsible for missing fathers and husbands.

Children feel just as lonely and empty as single parents. Having the extra burden of being blamed for the absence of fathers is a burden that we cannot shoulder. **Jason**

Women, in particular single parents, should instill in their young black sons, values that will prevent them from disrespecting women. They should instill in young black boys the idea that it is not ok to leave women to bring up children on their own. Most women leave their sons to repeat the mistakes of their absent fathers. Black women are successful now partly because of the values their mothers pass on to them; they should do the same for boys. I am not blaming our women for the problems the black community faces, but I do think black women should make more of an effort to make sure black boys do not repeat the mistakes of their missing fathers. **Anonymous**

Do you know there is a difference between love and sex in a man's mind?

I don't know what it is with women, but they get mixed up when it comes to sex. Sex is sex, love is love; there is no connection between the two for most men. In my experience women tend to think (wrongly) that if you have sex with them, you love them or want a relationship. It is about time women got the message-men like to fuck with anything or any one. We do not have to love you to fuck you. If I had a pound for every time a woman told me that she cannot do it with anybody, she has to care for them first, then I would be a rich man. If women want true equality then they must behave like men-enjoy sex and do not assume sex and love go hand in hand. **Clifford**

Women wrongly or rightly believe there is a connection between love and sex. If they have an intimate sexual relationship with a man they presume that the man cares for, or even loves them. If that is what they want to believe, so be it. For heaven's sake do not make the mistake of thinking men necessarily think the same way. I admit this is a generalisation: there are men who will not have a sexual relationship with someone, unless they care for them, and undoubtedly there are women who want sex and do not necessarily want, or expect love. Nevertheless, I have spoken to a number of male friends who all agree with me; they can happily have sex with a woman and not care for her in the slightest. If any woman does not believe me, then ask any man for yourself. **Anonymous**

If you (women) are having a sexual relationship with a man who you think loves you, and the only reason you think he loves you, is because he makes love to you, then don't believe he loves you until he shows you, tells you or makes a commitment to you. **Anonymous**

As a black woman, how would you like to see yourself in the world?

As black women how do you want to be seen by outsiders? As baby mothers, single parents, educated women or as thick and stupid. As martyrs or as capable, sophisticated women. What do you want your legacy to be as we approach the 21st century? **Oliver**

Why have the intimate and personal relationship between black men and women become more of an issue in the 1990s?

I would like to know why we started hating each other. In the words of Rodney King, 'Why can't we get along?' **Anonymous**

What is happening between black men and women in the 1990s? Why is it that we face more problems coming into the 21st Century than we faced in the last 100 years. We should be getting together. **Anonymous**

What do black women find attractive about white men that makes them want to go out with them?

How many times have you seen a well-dressed, elegant black woman with a tramp of a man from another race? I get the impression that these women want a non-black man so much that they are willing to accept anything. My question, therefore, is addressed to both black men and black women who go out with people from other races. I would like to know... why?

I doubt very much that the answer is simply love. Is it that you do not want your children to have nappy hair? Are you so brain washed that you believe light skin or straight hair is better than your own? What do you find so attractive about white or Asian men? **Lewis**

5 What do you think black women expect from black men?

ONLY black women can tell you what they want from black men. Nonetheless, it is interesting to discover if what black men think women want corresponds to what women actually want.

Some black men argue that women expect too much. They want an ideal that does not exist, never has existed and never will exist. On the other hand, some black men say so little has been delivered that they suspect black women expect very little from black men. The answer, I believe, lies some where between these two extreme views.

Too much (50 per cent)

Black women want too damn much. They want a man who is in touch with his feminine side, but at the same time they want a macho man. Women want a loving and caring man, but more often than not they ignore the caring man and turn instead to the rough man or the Mr. Smooth.

Women want to be treated as equals but still expect men to take the lead. They want to be treated with kindness. When you do treat them with kindness and show courtesy they see you as weak and soft, they take advantage and leave you for a man that will slap them around.

They want you to be more open with your feelings, to discuss whatever is on your mind. To do that is to destroy what makes you a man. Men are men. We are different from women. Women should not expect men to be more like women. **Conrad**

A Partner (10 per cent)

Not having spoken to many black women or being an expert on relationships, I guess black women expect the same things as women of all races: a partner to share their hopes and dreams. It is appaling and a damn fucking shame when 40% of young black men, between the ages of 18-32, go out with non black-women. I cannot think of any other race where such a large percentage of men disrespect and ignore their own women. It's a damn fucking shame to come out of slavery only to go back voluntarily with the oppressors. **Anonymous**

Women want companionship from a like-minded person. In short, women want a man. That is not as easy as it sounds when you consider that 40% of young black men reject black women. The figure is even higher if you add the black men who are gay or in prison. The pool of eligible black men is not all that. **Eddie**

It is reasonable to assume that black women expect black men to be with them. Personally, I do not think it is asking too much; it should be a right. **Elroy**

A man who is in work (10 per cent)

I guess black women would want a man who is employed or who is at least employable. You cannot expect them to want any less. At times, however, black men and black women are competing for the same jobs. What black women should realise is that they are used by white men to displace black men from jobs. If a white company has to hire a black person they will usually choose a black woman. Black men are still seen as a threat. It is not simply a matter of black men refusing to work; black women have to realise that at times the odds are stacked against us. **Robert**

Like the song said, 'Nothin' going on but the rent, you gotta have a J O B if you want to be with me. I will have to avoid you if you are unemployed'. Need I say more? **Anonymous**

Honesty, trust and respect (10 per cent)

They expect to be able to trust a black man. **Anonymous**

In the words of Aretha Franklin, 'R E S P E C T'. **Anonymous**

Black women expect at the very least to be treated with the respect that comes from being equal. **Dean**

Sisters expect respect. They want to be treated with the same respect that you would expect your mother to be treated with. **TR**

I suppose black women would like an honest and trustworthy man. In terms of trust, black women should learn to trust black men. **Anonymous**

Love and commitment (7 per cent)

If black women are to be believed, they are starved of love and commitment. I believe black women would go further and say love and commitment are two words absent from the vocabulary of black men. This being the case, then I guess they would expect love and commitment from black men.

You cannot love someone and not be committed to them. Black women should expect commitment from their men. Black women should also be prepared to walk away from a relationship if they are not getting what they want. Black women often expect but do not always demand.

It is one thing to expect, it is another to get what you expect. I expect to get a job after I graduate from university. I am not going to get the job unless I go for it and do not accept anything less. Black women sometimes accept less, and certain black men are more than happy to provide less than expected. **Anonymous**

Direction (5 per cent)

Black women expect direction from black men, direction in what to do and in setting an example. Women are good followers and men are usually good leaders. **Anonymous**

Women expect religious guidance and direction from men. **Ray**

One of the problems with black women is that they have been directionless for too many years. They have been alone for too long, doing what they please. Men did not care because it did not affect them too much. Now however black women are taking the wrong direction. Black women are heading in the direction men controlled for hundreds of years. It is now time for women to be directed back home and into the kitchen. **Anonymous**

Responsible fathers (5 per cent)

If there is an area in which black women and men should agree it is this. Irresponsible fathers not only affect black women. Irresponsible fathers affect black boys and girls. They destroy generations of boys and girls who will not get the guidance a responsible father can give and condemn generations of black women to a life of hardship, struggle, loneliness, and, at times, destruction. Therefore women want men who are not going to run away from their responsibilities in bringing up and looking after their children. **Anonymous**

Men who are proud of them and their race (1 per cent)

With the rise in the number of black men going out with white women, black women want black men who appreciate them for being who they are; descendants of a strong race with a history. **Abdul**

Black women want black men to be appreciative of their blackness. In that way black people will not have to play the colour game which includes desiring women of other cultures. **Anonymous**

Other (2 per cent)

I do not think black women expect anything from black men. After all, they are meant to have it all, independence, money, jobs and artificially created babies. Black men are now redundant. **Anonymous**

They expect great sex. A good sex life should keep them happy. **Kenneth**

Women expect men to provide money, more money and even more money. **Patrick**

All they want is our money. Money, money, money–that is all women expect. **Anonymous**

I cannot remember meeting a woman who did not want my money. They always use their femininity when it suits them, ie when money is involved. **RB**

PART TWO

Brothers on relationships

"A woman, in particular a black woman, should trust her man until he gives her reason not to. Black women often do not trust their men, not because of what they have done but because of what some other man has done or because they are told not to by white society, girlfriends or their mothers. A meaningful relationship cannot develop without trust."

"Women get treated the way they teach men to treat them..."

If a lie, presented as truth, is repeated enough times, by enough people, over a long enough period, people will eventually come to believe in that lie. In terms of black men and relationships, so many myths exist, that is it sometimes difficult for us to separate myth from reality, truth from falsehood, half truths from outright lies.

My intention is not to perpetuate the myths surrounding black relationships or to create new ones. However, certain points have to be made when dealing with relationships between black men and women. These issues are NOT peculiar to the black community; they also relate to other communities.

We as a community have an alarmingly large percentage of single parents. Marriage is not viewed by a significant percentage of black women and men as a prerequisite for parenthood. A large percentage of black men choose to date white women, an increasing number of black women are dating white men. A **large number** of black men do not take responsibility for bringing up their children.

The intention in this chapter is to bypass any political, theoretical, or ideological belief and simply give black men the opportunity to answer some of these points. I deliberately have not dealt with the issue of mixed relationships as I believe this deserves a book all of its own. I felt it was more important to concentrate my efforts on black-on-black relationships.

It is easy to overlook other aspects of black men's relationships with black women. This is why I covered other issues, from what couples argued most about, the best and worst places to meet a potential partner, the qualities men are looking for in a partner to why men cheat in relationships.

6 What advice would you give a black woman looking for a black man?

IF you want a prince you must act like a princess. A person with prince-like qualities is not going to marry, or be attracted to, a woman who is not dignified or who has not got princess-like qualities. Often women want qualities in men they themselves do not possess. If you want a good man, you have to be a good woman. Good men gravitate to good women.

Broaden your horizons

If I had to give black women advice, it would be this: know what you are looking for in a man and do not assume where you will find that special person. Often what you are looking for is right under your nose. Decent men come in packages you do not always want to unwrap. The fat guy you refuse to look at, the skinny guy you refuse to see, the guy who is not all that fine, the shy guy you walk past-all can be the princes you are looking for.

Women often turn down the chance of happiness because of the ridiculous criteria they use when looking for a partner. I am not advocating you to lower your standards; what I am suggesting is you consider ordinary hard-working men like myself. **Prince in waiting of a Princess**

Men will treat you the way you teach them to treat you

What I have noticed about black women over the years is that they rarely accept personal responsibility for choosing the wrong partner. They blame everybody but themselves for being, and remaining, in a bad relationship. If I had to give one piece of advice to a black woman it would be this: men will only treat you the way you teach them to treat you. Do not settle for less than you expect. If he treats you bad, leave him. If he cheats on you, leave him. If he abuses you physically or mentally, leave him. If he refuses to make a commitment, leave him. There are hundreds of thousands of black men in this country.

There are millions if you are prepared to look overseas.

Whatever you decide to tolerate in a relationship is what you will have to put up with. If you do not want it then do not take it. My friend constantly disrespects his woman. He tells her he is going to the shops and will be back in a few minutes. He returns ten hours later; in one instance he returned two days later, without so much as an explanation. The damn-fool woman accepts his behaviour. If he was going out with my lady, he would never dare do that because she would never, ever give him the opportunity to do it a second time. She would leave him. Men will only treat you the way you let them treat you. **Anonymous**

Know thyself first

If you are not comfortable with yourself, what are the chances that whoever you meet will be comfortable with you? Your first love should be yourself. Before you go off looking for a partner you should know what you have to offer. By taking the time to know yourself you develop inner confidence, increasing your chances of finding the right mate. **Adrian**

Make a list/know what you want

Without doubt the only advice I would give a black woman looking for a black man is to make a list. You certainly make a list when you are buying a car, a house or a major appliance. If you do not make a list when you are committing yourself to the purchase of major appliances, you certainly make a mental note of what you expect from the appliance. If it does not meet your expectations you leave it and move on until you find one that does. Why, then should things be any different when it comes to picking a partner?

I made a list of the characteristics that I wanted in a potential partner. More importantly, I measured myself against the list I prepared. I wanted a trustworthy, loyal and culturally aware woman. I knew I had these qualities. I also wanted someone who was open with their feelings. I am not very emotional therefore I wanted someone to bring out that side of me. Remember, you must have the courage to stick to your list, otherwise there is not much point making one. **Anonymous**

'Know what you want' is my advice to black women trying to find a black man. How do you know what you want? The answer can be applied to any area of your life, not just finding a partner. You find out what you want by making it up. It is that simple. The majority of people do not know what they want. They expect the answer to materialise magically. Well, it does not. You have to decide what you want. There are no rules. You decide want you want and then devise a plan to get it. When looking for a black man it is important to know what you want. If you do not know what you want you will end up with scum. You will also accept scum. **Anonymous**

Do not leave it to fate

If a black woman is looking for a black man she is on the right track. She is half-way there. She is looking. She has made a conscious decision to find a mate. She has not left it to fate. That, in my humble opinion, is the right thing to do. You want something. You go after it. Leaving it to fate is bullshit. If you want to go to university, you do not leave it to fate. You get the right qualifications and send in the application form. If you want to be a doctor, lawyer or crook you do not leave it to fate. You take steps to realise your dreams.

Relationships are no different. If you want a partner or if you want to get married, my advice is not to leave it to fate. Take steps to get what you want now. If you leave it to fate you may be waiting for years. I know of women who are still waiting for fate to deliver them a partner or a husband. When I ask women who are waiting for fate to deliver a husband what are they doing to get a husband they invariably say 'Nothing. I am just waiting for him to be delivered to me.' **Anonymous**

Make the first move if you have to

It is cool to approach a guy if you like him. That is my advice to a black woman looking for a black man. Why wait? We are, after all, approaching the 21st century. When I asked my wife why she approached me she said it was because she got tired of waiting. She also said it seemed to her that all the wrong guys approached her. For some reason, the men she really liked never seem to show an interest. Maybe they were intimidated by her looks and height. My wife is very pretty and very tall.

To be perfectly honest I was also one of the guys who was intimidated by her. I liked her when I first saw her. However, I assumed a pretty woman like her must have a boyfriend. I also assumed the stereotypical view that since she is good-looking she must be very standoffish and unapproachable. She was, in fact, the very opposite. My advice to women is not to be afraid to approach a man they really like. **Anonymous**

It is better to be alone than to wish you were alone

My grandmother told my mother many years ago, when she was about to divorce my father, that it is better to be alone than to wish you were alone. I believe this is sound advice. Whenever I am not sure about a woman I always remember that piece of advice. At that point I am not apprehensive about dropping someone I am not comfortable with. Therefore the only advice I would give to a black woman who is looking for a black man is the advice my grandmother gave to my mum. It is better to be alone than to wish you were alone. Love is not blind; always look before you leap. It is next to impossible to change an individual once you are going out with them. Sometimes it is better to be alone. **Anonymous**

Relationships are not the be-all and end-all

You can blame a black man for dragging you down. However, you have to blame yourself for staying down. My advice to women is to remember there are other things in life just as important as having a relationship. Do not be in a rush. Take your time. Pick the person you want to be with very carefully. If he has children with several women, chances are the brother does not know about commitment. So walk away. Keep looking until you find the right one.

In the mean time devote yourself to other things. Learn a new activity, go to college, spend money developing yourself, buy personal development books. How much money have you spent on your personal development in the last year? Join a keep fit-class, make new friends. Do the things you always wanted to do but kept putting off. The more you do with your life the less likely you will be to develop a dependency mentality. You will see you do not have to settle for a man who is not treating you right; or who is reluctant to make a commitment to you. **DF**

Other advice

Do not pre-judge and assume the worst. **Anonymous**

Be more open when approached by black men. You can lower your guard. **Gary**

In the words of Jesse Jackson, 'keep hope alive.' If your mind can conceive it and your heart can believe it, then you can achieve it. If you really want a decent man, never ever give up hope. The journey may be a long and lonely one, but you must believe there is a man out there for you. It is just a matter of time before your paths cross. Keep your eyes on the prize and it will be yours. In the meantime get on with your life. **Vernon**

Pray and ask God to find you the right one. **Anonymous**

Be patient, but if he is not willing to try as hard as you are then give him the boot. **Anthony**

Make sure you have your own money. **Anonymous**

Make sure the man you are after is sincere and committed to a monogamous relationship. If he is not, dump the bastard and get on with your life. **Anonymous**

Do not carry emotional baggage into a relationship. **Peter**

Do not stereotype black men. Treat us all as individuals. **Derek**

Look beyond the outside trappings and look inside the person. **Anthony**

All relationships are about give and take. No one person in a relationship should be giving too much or taking too much. **Anonymous**

Make sure he treats you right and looks after you. It is the least you deserve. **MH**

7 What qualities are black men looking for and expect from black women?

INTERESTINGLY, the vast majority of men did not concentrate on superficial factors. For instance, physical beauty or characteristics such as big and long legs/thighs, big breasts, big buttocks, or whether women were light or dark-skinned, short or tall, slim, fat or skinny. That is not to say men do not discriminate on the basis of these characteristics. But it shows that the majority of men realise that if you want a partner for life you have to look beyond the superficial. Relationships founded on superficial or physical characteristics seldom last, or they last as long as the superficiality can be maintained.

When choosing a mate one should look beyond superficial beauty and physical characteristics. More care should be devoted to other qualities. This brings me back to the original question. What qualities are black men looking for and expect from black women? Is it a woman who is not afraid of the kitchen, as one of the respondents said? Is it a like-minded companion, or someone who understands them?

In order of preference black men want the following qualities in black women.

Respect and understanding

Women are taught to disrespect men from the time they are girls. How many times have women said to their daughters, ' you cannot trust men to do anything'. That sort of attitude breeds disrespect. A lot of black men will privately admit to wanting a woman who will give them support and respect. **Anonymous**

Many women nowadays do not respect men. I do not mean that in a sexist manner. If a man shows you no respect you would be a fool to respect him. Women belittle men. If they are more successful they remind him of it and ask why he is not as successful as them. Being more successful than a man in career, education or finance is no reason to disrespect him.

I may not be working but I am still trying. I still want to be somebody. I want a woman who understands that the going is not always going to be good. Having understood that she must be prepared to stay with me and respect me. **Anonymous**

Trust and loyalty

A friend once said to me, 'what the eyes cannot see the heart does not feel.' The remark refers to trusting your partner. I believe if you cannot trust your partner you should not be in that relationship. I expect trust from any woman I date. It has become a cliche, but black women do not trust black men. I am so fucking tired of black women going on about how they cannot trust men. What do they think will happen if they do trust black men? **Anonymous**

If I cannot trust a woman, then the relationship can never grow. If she is late I would think the worst. If she goes out I would think she is seeing someone or doing something with somebody. If we go out and she speaks to someone I would think they are having an affair or about to have one. Often when men do not trust women they get very possessive and violent towards them. That is why I value trust in a relationship. I look for women who are worthy of being trusted and not just trustworthy. **JM**

Finance

It is a sad fact of life-but no romance without finance. I want a woman who can afford to contribute to the house. It is next to impossible to survive with only one bread-winner. You need two wages. I am not saying true love is dependent on your bank account. However, I am not interested in any woman who is not going to bring in a wage packet. **Anonymous**

Home-oriented

Women are so busy being career women that they have forgotten how to be domesticated. I want a black woman who still remembers her way to the kitchen. Any man who brings out a long list of what he wants or expects from a woman and doesn't mention domestics is a liar. **Anonymous**

I expect my woman to cook. I can do certain household chores like washing, cooking, cleaning and ironing-I would like a woman who has those qualities too. **Greg**

A woman is not a woman unless she knows her way to the kitchen and knows how to look after her house, man and children. **Nigel**

Self-reliance

I do not expect my partner to borrow my life. I want a woman who has some sort of independent life. I want her to share my interests and I expect us to have joint interests and do things together. That does not mean I want her to be with me 24:7. **Ade**

I do not want a woman so attached to me that if I sneeze she gets a cold. I want a woman who is willing to give me freedom in a relationship. Not freedom for me to do as I please, but freedom for me to develop and grow. Your life does not stop because you have met somebody. Life goes on. Remember, both of you had a life before you met. **Perry**

A good attitude towards my friends and family

It's great when a woman can joke and get on with friends who have stood by you through thick and thin. If a woman really wants to judge you, or find out what type of person you are, she has to look no further than your life-long friends. I would also expect a potential partner to fit in with my family. I am very close to my family, if a potential partner does not get on with my family we are unlikely to last long. **Darby**

Sexual compatibility

I want a woman who has an interest in sex and who does not see it as something dirty. **Anonymous**

I want and expect a woman who can satisfy me sexually. There is no point if one of you is very demanding and the other only wants to make love on Sundays. Sooner or later the one who is going without is going to find gratification elsewhere. Both women and men have said they would leave their partner if the relationship is good but the sex is lousy. **NB**

Ambition and intelligence

I want a woman who has the same level of ambition and intelligence as me. **Anonymous**

I do not want a woman who hates work or who is allergic to work. I want a woman who is hard-working and ambitious. **Lawrence**

Compatibility

She has to be compatible in terms of intelligence, interests, values and morals. My friend is with a very nice woman. The only problem is that she is too different from him. They argue about everything.

Whoever said opposites attracts should be shot. **Anonymous**

8 What are your tips for a long-lasting relationship?

THE romancing has come to an end. You get to learn about each other's bad habits. Second thoughts are beginning to creep in. You cannot believe this is the person you wanted to spend the rest of your life with. You sense trouble ahead. What do you do? What can you do? The following suggestions are offered by men who are still, or have been, in long term relationships.

Learn to communicate effectively

You must learn to communicate in a way that your partner understands. This is the most difficult skill to master in a relationship. Ironically, it is the most important skill to master if you want your relationship to work in the long term. You communicate not only through speech, but also through body language–ie posture, gesture, expressions and tone of voice. Body language and tone of voice have a greater impact when we are trying to communicate. In essence, it is not what we say but how we say it.

In relationships we tend to forget how to communicate. We shout, bully and manipulate and hope our partner understands the message we are trying to get across. It is not until the problem re-occurs that we realise the problem is still there.

Learn to communicate effectively. When you speak to your partner make sure she understands what you are saying. Often couples have problems and they have a different understanding of the problem. You must make sure the meaning you give to an event or the way you are interpreting what your partner is saying is correct. I changed the way in which I communicated with my girlfriend. I changed because I noticed that the meaning she was giving to the things that I did and said were not the meanings I gave to them. Now I explain myself. I make sure we both have the same understanding of the problem and its consequences. Effective communication will save you a lot of pain and heart break. **Efi**

You cannot find a solution until you have defined the problem. If you want your relationship to work in the long term you must speak out. If there is a problem you must point it out to your partner. Do not ignore the problem in the hope that it will go away. From experience I can tell you it does not. You must communicate any problems to your partner. It is a matter of short- term pain for long-term gain. **Carl**

There must be love

Love is the key So said Frankie Beverly and Maze. I wholeheartedly support this. No love, no relationship; certainly not a long-term one. If you love your partner you tend to stick around when the going gets rough, also you are more likely to want to make a go of it. The sacrifices do not seem so bad. I knew my partner did not love me, but because of circumstances and pressure we got married. Big mistake. Within 12 months we were both seeing other people. Within 18 months we were divorced. **MV**

There must be love, whole-body love for your relationship to work long-term. You must love the whole person. I know men are often parts men, which means they find a particular part of a woman's body more appealing than other parts. That mentality is fine in the short term, in the long term you must love the whole person.

The body parts we are attracted to can become liabilities in the long term. Big breasts can droop through weight gain or after childbirth. If you love only beautiful women that in itself can be a trap. There will always be a more beautiful woman, or someone may want your beautiful wife. What happens when she is no longer beautiful? Do you leave her for someone else? Light-skinned women may show signs of aging prematurely. If you are serious about developing a long-term relationship, then learn to love the complete person, warts and all. **Anonymous**

Commit yourself to the relationship

The first thing I would tell anyone who wants a long-term relationship is to be sure that is what they want. If you have to work on your relationship too hard it is not worth it. If you spend more time working on the relationship than enjoying it, maybe you should consider whether you are in the right relationship. If you are still looking at other women or men, or are not prepared to commit to one person then you are not going to make it in the long-run. Give your all and you will make it. **Anonymous**

Learn to compromise

My tip for the survival of any relationship is not to be too big to say SORRY, and always make up BEFORE you go to bed. Learn to compromise on certain issues. If your are not prepared to compromise in a long-term relationship, then get prepared for pain. It is as simple as that. No compromise, no happy relationship. Without compromise you will have a dictatorial relationship and even an abusive one. There are issues on which you will absolutely not give in. But the majority of arguments can be settled without bloodshed or the humiliation of either of those involved. **Anonymous**

Be realistic about the relationship

Most couples expect so much from a relationship that they invariably end up disappointed. My tip is not to expect too much. Have realistic goals for the relationship. If, as my partner expected, a replacement dad and to relive her childhood then the relationship is not going to work, as mine did not. Bear in mind that the more unrealistic the expectation the less likely the relationship will work. **Wayne**

Give each other space to grow

A relationship is only one part of your being. Do not make it the entire reason for your existence. Sometimes the saying 'absence makes the heart grow fonder' is true. I am not advocating that one or both partners disappear for days on end, but do find time to develop separate interests. You need to give each other space to grow and to develop into strong individuals. A relationship is more healthy that way. **Anonymous**

Make God the foundation of your relationship

We all need a helping hand at times. I have found the Man Upstairs is never too big to offer a helping hand. My tip for a long-lasting relationship is to have a third party present. Someone who is trusting, not prone to take sides. The third party is the Lord. He will provide answers and hope when you have given up all hope. **Anonymous**

With God's help everything is possible. In a society that is morally lacking, that actively encourages young people into dope and vice, you need a guiding light. Whether you are a black Muslim, born-again Christian, Methodist or Seven Day Adventist, you need a helping hand if your relationship is going to survive long term. **Jason**

Honesty and trust

Two of the most important ingredients a long-term relationship needs are trust and honesty. Without them you are left wondering about your partner, always thinking the worst. You are never quite sure where they have been or who with. To build a relationship without honesty and trust is like building a house without foundations. It is impossible. If you cannot trust your partner, leave them. **Anonymous**

Make quality time for each other

Often the first thing that is sacrificed in relationships is the time couples spend together. You are so busy with work and the children that it becomes impossible to find the time for each other. As a result you drift apart. That is what happened to my girlfriend and myself. It got to the point where the only time we spent together physically was in bed sleeping. That situation, thank God, has changed.

The secret is to find a balance with the 101 things you have to do. In a way you have to be superman or woman. You have to find time for yourself, time to be with your partner, time for the kids if you have any, and on top of that you have to deal with all of life's ups and downs. **Samuel**

Be friends and lovers

There are so many clichés when it comes to relationships, but many of them are true. One that is often used but seldom understood is your partner should be your friend as well as your lover.

What has kept my partner and I together more than nine years is the fact we are friends as well as lovers. We tell each other everything, often before we tell our respective best friends. Through the ups and downs we stayed together because we were friends and not just lovers. When the sex was bad, we understood because what we had was not based on sexual gratification. When the honeymoon was over and we saw each other in the raw, we understood. Through sickness,debt and raising children, we understood better than most because we are friends. A friend of mine once asked me if my wife was not my wife, would I choose to be her friend? The answer was yes, yes and hell yes. **Markus**

Do not take each other for granted

I took my long-standing girlfriend for granted until she walked out on me. In a long-term relationship do not take each other for granted. It is the easiest thing to do. You automatically assume she or he will always be there. Gradually you forget the birthdays, then the anniversaries, then your manners, then you come in all hours without explanation, then you expect your dinner on the table, so it goes until... she/he leaves your ass. I was lucky. I realised what I was doing. I apologised and made a serious effort to change. **Johnson**

Acknowledge each other in a long-term relationship. If he/she does something different or takes the time to do something special, then acknowledge it. It may be something small to you but it isn't to them. They did that little bit extra, and they expect at least to be complimented. **Anonymous**

Seek advice

Relationships are difficult at the best of times. They can be impossible when you have disagreements and endless rows. That is why it pays to have a trusting and neutral friend or family member to turn to for neutral advice. Someone who can guide both of you. Your relationship stands a greater chance of success if you can find a mediator. **ARC**

Do not expect your partner to meet all your needs

I wish I knew then what I know now. I read in a book that we should not expect our partners to meet all our needs. I believe this is the most important thing you need to understand in a relationship, long or short term. Self-worth, self-respect, confidence, security, morality come from within not necessarily from a partner. There are problems people carry with them that can never be solved by a partner. Not many couples are willing to accept that. We naturally look to our partner for the answer. If the answer or need is not met or fulfiled by our partners we feel our partner has let us down. As a result the relationship disintegrates.

As a result of feeling guilty and inadequate about not being able to meet my ex-girlfriend's needs we decided to split. In retrospect I realise I could not possibly have met all her needs; no one person could have. **Anonymous**

9 How do you recover from the break-up of your relationship?

MEN are not often, if ever told how to get over a relationship. Brothers below give a wide range of suggestions on how to recover from a broken relationship.

Analyse and move on

If we do not learn the lessons of the past we will repeat the same mistakes in the future. That is why I try to view the relationship from that of a third party. It does not take away the hurt, but it does stop you repeating the same mistakes over and over again. Viewing from a third-person perspective helps you see your mistakes. **NTG**

To get over a relationship I replay the relationship in my mind. I view it as if I was watching a film. I Analyse my contribution as honestly as possible, without bias. Did the relationship end because of something I did? Did I have the right mental attitude? Next I analyse my ex's contribution. What part did she play? What can I learn? Is there anything I can, or should do, in the future to avoid the same mistakes. Never wallow in self pity. **Vance**

Evaluate your life

I believe that if any man, after the break up of their relationship, evaluates their life, they will see that they have put off a lot of things they wanted to do. The best way to get over your partner is to do all the things you had planned to do before you met.

When I broke up with my girlfriend I found that I had not done half the things I wanted to accomplish. I remembered I always wanted to write, so I took writing up. I had neglected my friends during the relationship, so I took the time to get reacquainted with them. Do not waste your energy by hating her or wishing her bad. Make a list of the things you want to do and tick them off as you accomplish them. By the time you get half way down the list you would have forgotten her. **AH**

Don't forget the good times

Once you have accepted that the relationship is over and that you will not be getting back together start to focus on the positive aspects of the relationship. I am not saying you should not review the bad parts, just don't dwell on negativity for ever. **Anonymous**

Someone once asked me to concentrate on the good times I spent with my partner. At the time I thought he was fucking crazy. I thought concentrating on the good times would only make me want her back. It did for a while. Looking back, however, I realise that concentrating on the good times helped me to get over my ex. I did not feel totally worthless or used when I concentrated on the good times. The negative consumes you with anger, bitterness and rage. These emotions make it harder to get over the relationship. **Anonymous**

It shall pass

A female friend once told me, 'don't worry this too shall pass'. So here I am four months later, waiting for the hurt to pass. **Mike**

I have not got any great strategy for getting over a relationship. Over the years I have been in a few relationships that did not work out. I got over the break-up with the passage of time. Time is a great healer, or at least helps you forget the person. **Rupert**

Yes, cry if you need to

If it hurts bad enough, cry. In private. Alone in a dark room. Cry a little pray a lot; you will soon get over her. **Anonymous**

Cry. It helps at times to cry. It will not help in all cases, but it does help in some cases. **Henry**

Keep looking

I have yet to find a way to get over a relationship completely. You think you have, then you see her with someone else and it hurts a bit. **Malcolm**

10 If you are in a relationship, what do you argue most about?

WHAT, then, do couples argue about? Are you kidding? Couples argue about everything from his annoying habits to her unruly friends. On a more serious note, the topic men said they argued most about in a relationship was money. In particular, how best to spend it; how there is not enough of it; how one or the other partner spends too much. Couples also argued about who controls the money coming in; how much to put away; how much they would like to put away and the reasons they are not meeting their target.

Other economic arguments focus on not having enough money to go out as often as they want to, or not going out at all because they cannot afford to. Not buying clothes or general shopping because of financial constraints or not being able to maintain the standard of living they enjoyed before they met their partners were issues also mentioned by men.

The other bone of contention is time spent apart. On the whole, men thought women always wanted them around and did not want them to go

out. Some of the men claimed that their girlfriends arranged joint activities although they knew their partners would be away. For example, they would be out on a Sunday playing football or cricket or engaged in some other regular activity.

Men also noted that they often argued with their partners about the number of times they go out together.

My girlfriend always wants me to take her somewhere. We can never go out enough. **VA**

The number of times she tells me I never take her anywhere! Once she says those words I know an argument is inevitable. **Jermain**

I think my partner's favourite words are, 'you never take me anywhere' or ' you never take me when you go out with your friends'. Another variation is 'we don't go out as often as before'. **Keith**

Other issues mentioned were the rules and boundaries of what is acceptable and unacceptable behaviour within the relationship. For example, having an ex-partner call, or the times at which his children from a different relationship can visit.

Sex, the amount of work done in the house, and what programmes they should watch on TV were also mentioned.

I argue with my partner about sex-I don't get any. **SS**

We argue a lot. With sex, we make love depending on her mood. It sometimes seems she punishes me by withdrawing sex and rewards me by giving me sex. I hate that. Sex should not be like that. **Lyndon**

We argue about general things-leaving the toilet seat up, wetting the floor, not always cleaning the bath, not cooking enough, or at all. Not putting up a shelf. Forgetting birthdays, her own and the family's. Who should be responsible for x and y. General stuff, some serious, some not too serious. **David**

11 Where is the best place for single black women to meet single black men?

THE million-dollar question: if you are single and looking for a partner where do you go to find that special person? Wait for it! The answer, according to black men, is anywhere and everywhere. The solution is not as vague as you may think. If you go through your day in your mind, you will see you come into contact with black men as soon as you open the door. The problem, then, is not where to meet single men but rather how you approach them and whether you want to take the chance of approaching a complete stranger.

The question is not so much the best place to meet single black men; rather it is what you are willing to do to meet single men. Do you give the right signals, are you approachable, do you take the initiative or do you sit back and hope? The answers to these questions will determine whether you will meet someone. **BJ**

If a black woman is having trouble finding eligible black men then maybe she should widen her pool by looking in other countries. Different ethnic groups already do this. There are millions of single black men in Africa, America and the West Indies. **Dennis**

I met my partner through a singles party organised by a friend. My friend had a party and asked everyone to bring someone who was single. The men brought male friends they knew were genuinely single and looking for a partner, the women did the same. It was an eventful and fun evening. **Mervin**

The best place to meet single and decent men is at church. People often say church is the best place to meet people, and I agree. However, if you go to church for the sole purpose of meeting a mate you may be disappointed. **Everton**

The best way to meet single men is through your mum. Get your mum to ask her friends if they know of any free men (or women). Believe me, it works. Your parents or grandparents usually have friends, other mothers and grandparents who know of single grown-up adults. **Anonymous**

The best place is through organisations that specialise in bringing single people together. They hold special dinners and dances all over the place. **Patterson**

Obviously, if you are single and looking for a single man it makes sense to go where single men go–Sunday league football/cricket, general sporting events and, of course, anywhere women go. Men are attracted to women. I go to events that I think would attract women. Single women need not look too far. **Anonymous**

Through friends. My friend introduced me to my present girlfriend. **Anonymous**

Some of the fittest men can be found in gyms up and down the country. You can find a man and get fit at the same time. Get yourself to a gym; there are literally hundreds of sports clubs you can join. You can do anything from martial arts to bowling, squash to badminton. **Sam**

The best place to meet a single black man is at social gatherings, especially weddings. **Ade**

The best place to meet someone is where people who are like you go. If you like church, then maybe it will be connected to a religious event or concert. If you are a student, then maybe at a college or university. **Joel**

At a carnival, a concert or even the cinema. **Jobrah**

Go to public places on your own. That is the way I met my girlfriend. After we had dated for a year or so she told me she read in a magazine that men are more likely to approach women who are on their own in a public place. Since I approached her and asked her out I guess the article was correct.

I should note that she attended safe places where there were hundreds of people. It took time for her to get the courage to do this. **Anonymous**

The place where 43% of black men meet non-black women is the best place for single black women to meet single black men. **Anonymous**

12 Where is the worst place for a single black woman to meet single black men?

WITHOUT doubt, hundreds of black men agree, the worst place for a black woman to meet a black man is at a night-club. It is ironic that a place with so many single people should be regarded as the worst place to meet a partner.

Clubs are the worst place to meet a single man. There are probably hundreds of single men there, but it is so dark and noisy you do not get a chance to see or hear anybody. **BM**

In night-clubs women carry on like they are too nice; like their shit don't smell. They have their faces all screwed up. Irrespective of how you approach them for a dance they still say no. The worst ones are the West Indian ladies. They never dance with African men. **Anonymous**

Black clubs are funny; you get women on one side, men on the other and neither of them ever mingle. **Anthony**

With black clubs nobody talks. Single men look at single women all night long and never strike up a conversation. It would be funny if it was not so pathetic. **Anonymous**

I do not have to explain why clubs are the worst place to meet a partner. Nobody talks. All single people stick to themselves and the people they come with and wonder, 'why I am going home alone; last time I come to this club'. In two weeks time they return-still no joy. **Patrick**

People come to clubs to enjoy themselves, see what they can pull for the night. So maybe the atmosphere is not the best for meeting people. **Jermain**

The place where 43% of black men meet non-black women is the worst place for single black women to meet single black men. **Anonymous**

A VD clinic is the worst place to meet someone single. **Anonymous**

At a bus stop. **AI**

At a gay benefit dance. Or a blues dance. It's too dark to see anyone. **BU**

In a betting shop. **PA**

In a white club. The black men who go there are after white women. The black women who are there are after white men. Have you noticed that the black people who go to predominantly white clubs never make eye contact with other black people in the club? **Anonymous**

13 Why is there a reluctance on the part of some black men to get married?

Lack of expectation on the part of both men and women

This question is stupid as far as I am concerned. My parents were not married. A lot of the people I know, their parents are not married. So why the hell should I get married? **Anonymous**

Black women do not want to get married. They are perfectly happy to have kids outside of marriage. Why stir trouble with this question? **Anonymous**

Coming from the West Indies, I have noticed something peculiar to black women born in Britain: some black women do not expect to get married. They expect to have children and be single parents, but for whatever reason they do not expect to get married. It is like someone eradicated the word marriage from their vocabulary. I will agree that in the West Indies we have our share of black men not marrying. However, unlike in Britain you do not have to search high and low before you find married couples.

From the many conversations I have had with black women since I have been in this country, I can say that many black women do not expect black men to marry them. As a result they are resigned to not getting married. We are left with a situation where neither party expects to get married, thus creating a self fulfiling prophecy. **Bradley**

There is a sort of apathy on the part of black men and women. If you talk about marriage to some of our young men and women they look at you as if you are mad. **Anonymous**

In my line of work I come into contact with a lot of young black boys and girls. One of the boys I once spoke to laughed in my face when I asked him if he would get married. His response was, "what is marriage?" If we have got to the point where our young boys and girls are asking what is marriage, then God help us. **Jason**

...In short the problem lies with both men and women. As long as women allow men to get away with not marrying them; men will be happy not marrying women. You have a situation where women blame men for not making the commitment. Men, on the other hand, will blame women for not expecting or demanding marriage. It is a little like the chicken and the egg argument. Which came first? **Anonymous**

Economic Factors

I cannot afford to get married. When you consider the amount of money it takes to get married and to stay married, it is not surprising that so many black men choose not to get married. There is a direct link between the economic well-being of black men and the rate of marriage and the large number of single female parents. If black boys leave school unqualified and subsequently cannot find work, what do you think are the chances of those unqualified black boys (who are now men) getting married or of them finding the money to support a family?

The rate of unemployment among black men is the highest of any ethnic group. The figure is likely to go up as many black boys leave school without even a basic level of education. Consequently, a higher number of black men will not view marriage as a serious proposition.

I believe this scenario can be averted by making sure black boys leave school well qualified to join the work force. We as a community should start creating and generating our own jobs. How many shops that sell black products are actually owned by black people? We give our wealth to other ethnic groups. We seem happy to let other people exploit us while we stay impoverished. I believe the economic situation of black men will determine whether or not they get married. You have to have money to be married. The truth is that, like thousands of black men, I cannot afford to get married. **Paul**

Seeing marriage as an end not a beginning

Some men have a fear of being held down. They have no willingness or desire to change. Therefore they see marriage as being stuck with the same person irrespective of whether the woman is right for them. **JD**

To be married to a woman means you have to be committed to her. You have to be with her only. In reality, some black men are just not willing to make that sacrifice. This type of black men are nothing less than fools. They are always chasing elusive rainbows. **Anonymous**

Commitment scares a lot of people, black men included. Commitment means giving up women and having just the one. Commitment means taking responsibility for your wife and children, providing financially, emotionally and physically. Some black men are just not manly enough to be committed. **Anonymous**

Following the lead of others/poor role models

My mum was a single parent. My view is that if you are raised by a single parent one of two things will happen. Either you get married when you get older because you do not want to be a bastard like your dad. He stayed single until he died, despite having three kids with two different women.The other option is that you become a bastard like your dad and do as he did-not get married or take responsibility for your actions. You just drift from one woman to the next, fucking them all up. **Andrew**

I have no role models. I do not know how to be married. That is why I have not got married. As long as we as a community tolerate single parents, then some black men and women will never get married. The definition of madness is to do the same thing but expect a different result. We must be mad because we do the same things and expect a different result. For instance, how many families go generation after generation having kids out of wedlock. Children are socialised into accepting the normality of single parent headed-households. **Anonymous**

Although I am very happily married, I found your question rather interesting. I asked several of my single black male friends why they are not married. The most popular answer was because their parents were not married. This attitude creates a never-ending vicious cycle. The attitude is, ' I am not going to get married because my dad was not married to my mum.' So it goes on with a new generation saying the same thing. **NP**

Other

The quality of black women leaves a lot to be desired. I doubt very much I would find a suitably qualified black woman in this country. I may have to go back home to find a wife. **Anonymous**

I am not married because I choose not to marry. I am sure I am not the only one who has come to that decision. **ABT**

I want to have a career before I consider marriage. **Anonymous**

We are approaching the 21st century. No one expects you to get married. **Anonymous**

14 Why are a high percentage of black women single parents?

A number of the men questioned noted what they saw as the 'martyr' complex of many black women when it comes to the issue of single parents and, in particular teenage pregnancy. The view expressed was that birth control is too advanced for the black community to tolerate such a high rate of single and teenage mothers. This places a great deal of responsibility on women to safeguard themselves against pregnancy but fails to take into account the role of black men in getting black women pregnant.

Some of the answers given by black men may appear to be excuses. It should be remembered however, that the men who took part in the survey came from different backgrounds. Some were married, others were absent fathers, some were single, others were living with, but not married, to their partners. The status of these men may have a bearing on the answers given. For example, an absent father may try to justify his absence so as to excuse his behaviour. A married respondent may be over-critical or hostile to the concept of single parents.

Socialisation

The basic rule of parenting is that children do as you do not as you tell them. Therefore, we have a situation in the black community where children repeat the behaviour patterns of their parents. If their parents are single, then chances are they will also be single parents. If you, or any person who reads this book disagrees, then please tell me why we have generation upon generation of single headed households? **Anonymous**

In the black community we have reached the dangerous ground where black women are expected to be single parents. Black men have reached the stage where they are not afraid to get a woman pregnant and simply walk away. That attitude and mentality is passed down to young boys and girls. Therefore, you have a mentality and a culture that encourages single headed households. **WY**

Single parents breed single parents.Young boys and girls are simply following the example set by their parents. **Anonymous**

The problem lies partly with men

The majority of single households are headed by women. I fully accept that the blame lies with black men. I also accept that without the strength of black women there would be no black family. I would like to take this opportunity to thank black single female-headed households for the job they have done. I am not being patronising. I am the product of a single household. Without the sacrifices my mum made, including going without, in order to send us to school, I doubt very much I would have been in a position to attend university.

Your question begs another question. If black women can make the sacrifice to bring up a family and, at the same time, work full time, why can't the black male community do the same? The black men who do not take care of their women and children are fucking cowards. They are weak. They are nothing more than boys playing at being men. They do not deserve to be alive. In view of the sacrifices black women have made and continue to make it is impossible to have any respect for any black man who does not support his children.

If you do not want children, at the very least you should act responsibly, for instance, wear condoms when having sex, or alternatively make sure the woman is using some form of birth control. If you do not want to have children, you do not have to. Birth control is there to prevent pregnancies. It is near enough 100% safe. You can have sex to your heart's content once you take preventative measures to stop the woman getting pregnant. **ST**

The majority of single parents are women. Men are the missing piece in this jigsaw, therefore some of the blame has to rest with men. Many men never pass the stage of being boys. Physically they are grown up; mentally they have not past the age of 16. You see these men everywhere, forever trying to be the player, forever trying to be young, free and single. They are blind to reality. They will never own up to responsibility; they do not know how to. I know this for a fact after speaking to my brother, who at 27, with two kids, refuses to provide for them or acknowledge their existence. **Anonymous**

Unfortunately, a lot of brothers are not responsible enough to look after a family. The question is why are they not responsible? Find out what keeps a brother from taking responsibility for his children and you may solve the problem of missing fathers. **MK**

Some men can be fools. I was going to say they have a slave mentality, but that would be doing an injustice to slaves-slaves took care of their women and children. These types of men are sick and have no morals. They equate manhood with how many women they can get pregnant. Although it is only a very small percentage of black men who who view manhood in this way, these men do exist and account in part for why we have single parents. They do not care about women or children. I often wonder why women go for these types of men. **Anonymous**

It is simple; you want to be a man have a baby. But if you want to be a real man, leave the baby mother to bring up the child on her own. **WA**

I once watched a single parent-family outing at McDonald's. The mum, a black woman, who I hardly knew, was a single parent. Something about watching them stirred an angry reaction within me. I was angry that she had to bring up children on her own. Black men should not be made to shirk their responsibilities.

Some black men are fucked up. They are quitters and cowards. They have no moral values. They are depraved. They cannot see the beauty in being there for your children. They cannot understand the notion of being responsible for your actions. They cannot understand that they are needed by their children and their woman. As far as they are concerned sex is only a means of physical gratification, a way of enjoying themselves. That is why they go from woman to woman. The consequence of sex is never thought of. **Anonymous**

Women are also to blame

It takes two to tango. It is futile pointing the finger of blame at men. Women are not passive creatures being sexually exploited by men. A lot of people would like to place the blame for single parents squarely at the doorsteps of men. That is wrong. For one thing, women have a choice. They choose the men they sleep with. They even have a choice as to whether to keep the baby or not. Secondly, birth control is very advanced. If you do not want to get pregnant, you do not have to. In the debate on single parents, women have to question their role and at times their motivation for having children.

Some women still believe–I stress some–they can get a man by having his child. These women should take a look around them and realise this does not work. If you want to trap a man, have him marry you. **JC**

Some black women like being single parents. That is why we have so many single parents. If black women do not want to be single parents they do not have to be. They can, for instance, refrain from having sexual intercourse until they are married. Also, they can stop getting pregnant by men who have two or three kids with different women. They can have an abortion. They can stop and think and learn the lessons of the past, instead of repeating the mistakes of their mothers. They can make better choices in picking male partners.

The debate concerning single parents is not complete unless we look at it from all sides. Yes, men have to take responsibility. Women also have to accept responsibility for the decisions they make. **Errol**

Some women want children but want nothing to do with the fathers. They make the choice to remain single. **HG**

Some black women feel more secure rearing children on their own. **Barry**

Some women are stupid. They believe that because they are having a sexual relationship with a man this means he cares. They only find out the truth when they get pregnant and he is no longer interested. Black women like being a martyr. I cannot understand why black women enter into a sexual relationship without either taking precautions against pregnancy or if they are expecting to get pregnant, why not first get the man to make a solid commitment. **Anonymous**

Boy, as far as I am concerned, women give birth. We have a high level of single parents because black women want it that way. They are very happy being single parents otherwise they would exercise greater control over their bodies. **Anonymous**

Conspiracy of silence in the black community

There is a conspiracy of silence in the black community that permits and tolerates, single-parent families. As long as we as a community stay silent the worse the problem will get. The number of single households have risen to the point where it may seem controversial to want to tackle the problem. What has happened in the last few years is that instead of tackling the problem of single parents we have developed reasons to excuse and justify it. Everyone turns a blind eye. The attitude of too many black people is that if we ignore the problem it will go away. If it is not discussed then it does not exist. **Anonymous**

The black British community does not condemn or attach any stigma to single parents. In order to change we need to go back to the old days when a finger was pointed at single parents. Prominent black people have to take a stand. As a community we have to say it is not acceptable for us to have such a high percentage of singe parents.

I am the product of a single-parent family. I am proud of my mother. She raised five children after my dad left us. I do not blame single parents for the ills of the world. I do not believe you will necessarily turn out to be a bad and unproductive member of society because you were brought up by a single parent. However, from personal experience I say a child needs both parents. The black men who keep producing and the black women who keep allowing men to get them pregnant: your day of judgment will come. My answer applies just as much to your question on marriage as it does to single parents. **Anonymous**

A generous welfare system

There are a lot of single parents because the welfare state is a good father. It provides money for nothing. It looks after the kids from birth till they leave home. It even provides more money if you remain single and have more children. Some women that are single parents have no ambition or education to lift themselves up off the fringes of society. They stay single parents because they know social security will provide for their kids. **Trevor**

You have a housing system that rewards single parents. Some girls choose this way to obtain a council house. Get pregnant and you are housed. **Anonymous**

Sex-and-no-responsibility culture

The message to our youth, who more often than not are the single parents, is that it is cool to have sex. We live in a bump and grind era. R & B, rap and ragga all encourage young people to be promiscuous. They glamourise sex. These songs all talk of freaking you, knocking the boots, tight needle eye, getting up, getting down, sex me, play me etc. Not one encourages black youths to be responsible about sex, or warns of the possible consequence of knocking the boots. **Derrick**

Circumstances

Not every relationship is going to work despite the best of intentions of both parties. Single parent mothers may be the result of divorce, as in my case, separation or even the death of a partner. One partner may choose to remain single. In the black community we tend to lump everyone in the same basket, which is wrong. In every single household there lies an individual story. **Marsel**

Other explanations offered centred on economics, for example, someone said that men are usually missing because they cannot provide financially. Other argument focus on role models, and repeating the mistakes of the previous generation; points already made in the answers relating to marriage.

15 If you have had an affair, why and how did it happen?

WITHOUT doubt this was one of the most difficult questions to get men to respond to. I had to gain the trust and confidence of the men I interviewed before they would open up to me. You will have to judge for yourselves if any lessons can be drawn from the stories which follow. I doubt very much that there is an adequate explanation for why men like Anthony who profess to love their wife and who are very happy in their relationship still feel the need to have affairs.

All names have been changed.

I am in my mid-thirties. I have a very well-paid job with a London council. I have been married for eight years and have two daughters. My wife and I have a solid relationship.

I had an affair with a work colleague. She worked on a different floor to me but we saw each other every day, always for work-related reasons. She was single. She knew I was married.

It started off innocently enough. I asked Claudette out to lunch. I asked her mainly because I was bored and did not want to stay in the office. I also was not in the mood to eat the sandwiches I had prepared for lunch. I enjoyed our first lunch date together, so I asked her out again. Before long we went out for lunch every day.

She had moved into a new house a month before. During a lunch break she had gone into a DIY store and bought replacement doors for her bathroom and two of the bedrooms. After work she asked if I could bring the doors to her house-her car was too small. I agreed.

After delivering the doors upstairs I was on my way out. I called out to Claudette. She came down wearing her robe. As soon as I saw her I felt my dick stiffening. I knew the best thing to do was leave. I could not. For the past month, although I hadn't said anything to Claudette I had watched her every move. The outline of her knickers. Her nipples through her top. I had even wondered what it would be like to fuck her.

Claudette approached me. I stood there. This is wrong. Please go home to your wife, I kept saying to myself. I could not move. I tried to move again; still I could not.

She started to undo my tie. I grabbed her. Ripped off her robe. Lay her on the carpet and made love to her. In truth, I fucked her. There was no tenderness. It was wild. It was lustful. It was great. Mainly it was lust.

I could not at first bear to confront my wife. I felt guilty. I knew I had betrayed her. I knew the right thing to do was to tell my wife. I could not tell her.

Why did I do it when I was very happy with my wife? The reason is that men can quite easily separate love from sex. When men cheat it is often for sex. They do not necessarily want a relationship with the other woman.

In retrospect, I think it was lust. Claudette and I made love at every opportunity-at work in the office basement where the dead files are kept. In the car. Even once in the park very late at night.

The relationship ended when Claudette applied for a higher paying job with a different council. It just fizzled out.

The affair happened two years ago. I regret it happened–all the more so since my wife is such a loving wife. There is not much I can do about it now. I want my family. I will never have an affair again. Therefore I have given up the idea of ever telling my wife what happened. **Anthony**

I am 26. I am single and an expectant father. I currently work for a high street bank. I recently broke up with my girlfriend of more than seven years. The woman who is expecting my child I hardly know. She is not my girlfriend. Not all couples who have problems with their relationship react by having an affair-just the foolish ones like me. I was going through a rough patch with my girlfriend-the type you think will never end, where you cannot bear to go home because you just know you will have a row.

On one such night, instead of going home I went out with a few friends to a wine bar. After that we went on to a club. Although I had a few drinks I was not drunk or even close to being drunk. I knew what I was doing. I met this woman. She was not my type, but we got talking. I went back to her place that night and we ended up in bed. I must have been seeing Shereen for a couple of months when she rang my girlfriend at work and told her she was pregnant with my baby.

My girlfriend did not believe her at first. She confronted me. She asked me if it was true. I said it was. I said that I was sorry. I did not mean to do it . It just happened. This woman did not mean anything to me.

'I love you and you only,' I pleaded. No use. I doubt very much she heard anything I said. I have never in my life seen anyone so hurt and destroyed, her dreams so utterly shattered.

Why did I do it? I could say it was because of the problems we were having. You tend to be weaker mentally when there are problems with your relationship. In that state I know men are sometimes more likely to have affairs.

We were having problems because of me. My girlfriend wanted to get married. We were getting old. We had being going out for a few years. We had been living together for two or three years.

I was not keen on getting married. Marriage seemed too final. I wanted to be young and free. Marriage scared me, so I reacted badly.

I picked unnecessary arguments. I teased her and provoked her. It became so bad that I did not want to come home. I did not want to talk about plans of getting married.

When I went to that club and picked up a woman who is so very different to what I am accustomed to, I was making a statement. I was still free. I can do as I please. There was no reason to continue seeing her. It should have only been a one-night stand. I became so careless that I had unprotected sex. That was so irresponsible of me. I could have got a sexual disease. I sometimes wish I had.

I think the baby is mine. I am not sure. My life is in ruins. I have lost a woman I loved very much. A woman who I promised on her 19th birthday I would build a dream home for. Somewhere along the way I forgot the promises I made. I wish I could be with her. I would marry her tomorrow if she ever finds it within herself to forgive me.

The affair cost me my house, my woman, my life. I have also destroyed a very magnificent black woman. I intend one day to get back with my girlfriend. I do not know how long it's going to take, but I pray everyday that she forgives me. I intend to build her that dream home. **Patrick**

I am in my thirties. I have been working for a number of years. I am at the moment contemplating leaving my job to set up my own business. I have been with the same woman for the past 15 years. I have had numerous affairs. As a child I never really felt loved. I find it very difficult to express love to anyone. I am not at all emotional and rarely show any emotion. I have only mentioned these points because I think they may have some bearing on why I am the way I am.

Within three years of meeting my partner I had my first affair. I had an affair with a woman at the firm I used to work at. Her name was Clarice. She was tall. She had a boyfriend. I believe they were on the verge of splitting up. She also had a child with him.

Clarice and I seemed to have so much in common. We clicked. We started seeing each other within a month of her joining the firm. At first it was strictly a sex thing between us. Over the years, however, it developed into more. She wanted me. I, on the other hand, did not want to leave my partner.

Clarice and I saw each other for over four years. Once she called me at home asking to see me. When I finally managed to get away I drove to her house. She had broken up with her boyfriend by then. She shared the house with her daughter.

She was crying when I arrived. She said there was something she had to tell me. She explained she had had an abortion. She said she had done it because she did not want any more children and because she wanted her child to have a relationship with its dad. I was not in a position to do that. I did not say much. I understood why she had done it. I think I would have left my partner if she had told me she was pregnant. But I said nothing to her. We cuddled and said very little for the entire night.

The relationship was never the same again. Within a year we stopped seeing each other. She said she had had enough. She could not see me again. She had to sort out her life.

I have seen at least 15 women since the break-up with Clarice. I have maintained my relationship with my partner. The reason for having affairs is that I have a strong desire to be loved. I do not necessarily want to love but I want to be loved. When I have an affair I feel loved in the early stages. But I do not know how to love. I do not know how to be committed to one woman. I do not even know if I love my partner who I have been with for many years. I have lost count of the number of times I have lied to my partner.

With the exception of Clarice, I have never felt anything for any of the women I have had affairs with. That is another reason I have affairs. This may be a generalisation, but women are ruled by their feelings; men are not. Since we are not ruled by our feelings we do not have a problem with having affairs. We are programmed that way. We were made to spread our seeds.

That is my story. I am sure readers of your book will not like me or care for me. What they should remember is that I am searching for love. I am trying to find the impossible. I am trying to find that child that was left alone crying and craving for attention. I am trying to find that teenager who was abandoned by his parents. I am trying to find myself. **Frederick**

I am 25 years old. I work for a civil service department. I am 6 feet 2 inches tall and weigh 13 stones–all muscle. My head is clean-shaven. I work out, play sports, and I am one of the best dancers you are likely to meet. I am dark-skinned. There is one more thing you should know about me-I love women. I have a steady girlfriend, nothing serious.

I first had an affair with a woman I met on the train. I was 21, she was 29 and engaged. We got the same train to work every day. Without fail she was always on the 7.46 train. However, it was more difficult to meet her on the journey home because she left work at various times. It was difficult but not impossible.

Her name was Shanice, she was light-skinned, about 5 feet 8 inches tall, flat chested and extremely good looking. She had a big ass for her size. She was slim with full juicy black people lips.

We got talking by accident. The train was cancelled. I decided to drive to the nearest Underground station. We had seen each other at the station for the past few months. So in a way we knew each other. I asked her and two other people who I knew in passing if they wanted a lift to the Underground station. They said yes. That is how I got talking to her.

At times I wish the train had been a few minutes late because I knew it would be full and that her ass would press against me. That is how I knew she was interested in me. The first time it happened took me by surprise and I got an erection when her ass touched my front. I was embarrassed. I tried to think of something that was not sexual. It did not work. I just got harder and harder. I could not get out of that train fast enough. I felt so embarrassed.

Her boyfriend, who I barely knew, was away for a few days. She invited me to her house. We made love every day he was away. She had the longest legs I have ever seen. I kissed her from her toes to her lips. I made love to her in every way possible.

I had the affair because I wanted Shanice. It was strictly sexual attraction. That was the reason for both of us. Women cheat just as much as men. Men do not have affairs with themselves. They have affairs with women who more often than not also have partners of their own. As far as I know Shanice is still with her boyfriend.

The truth is there are as many reasons for having affairs as there are men having affairs. Each person who has an affair has his own way of justifying it. I love women. I just cannot seem to keep away from them. **Randolph**

I am a professional working for a relatively small, conservative firm which caters for high- powered clients. I am living with my partner. We have been dating for rather a long time. I am having an affair with a placement student at my firm.The members of staff do not know or suspect anything. I suppose it would never cross their minds that a British Afro-Carribean would be having a homosexual affair with an Asian.

When I met my girlfriend I was still a virgin. I was in my early twenties. I always knew I was gay but I never had the courage to do anything about it. I suppose Ahmed changed all that. I do not see myself having a long-term or serious relationship with Ahmed. However, the affair is a first step to becoming what I truly am. Looking back, I believe I had the affair to see whether I really preferred men. Although I had planned to get married to Gemma, I believe I no longer will. I have decided to tell her I am gay and therefore cannot continue the relationship. **Jason**

I am fast approaching 40. I have two children with my partner, who I have been living with for the past 18 years. We are not married. I work for a transportation company.

I am very interested in why people have affairs. For me the reason for having affairs is simple: I love black women. I cannot commit myself for the rest of my life to one woman. Some of my friends have been married for ten years or more. I know of many black men who are disgusted by my behaviour. These black men have never cheated. My brother has been married for many years and he has never cheated on his wife as far as I know.

What interests me about affairs is why people like me do it and someone like my brother does not. The answer I have found is respect, commitment, maturity, discipline and acceptance. If you respect your woman you are not going to fool around. If you respect her you are not going to make her look a fool by having people know what you are doing. Commitment means accepting one woman through good and bad times.

It takes maturity to realise that you cannot have all the women in the world, to look at women as equals and not as potential sexual conquest. You also need the discipline to say no. The final and most important ingredient is acceptance, acceptance that you are doing wrong.

The majority of men who have affairs do not think they are doing anything wrong. This is for a number of reasons. Firstly, they often do not love the woman they are having the affair with. Therefore there is no emotional/mental betrayal of their partner. That makes all the difference to men. Secondly, it is only a sex thing. Thirdly, the affair can be justified.

Most affairs fulfil a need for men-a need to be loved, a need for physical gratification, a need to reassure one's ego, a need to be with women, a need to be wanted and feel appreciated, a need to escape from one's wife or girlfriend.

My friends asked me why I don't leave my partner and then I can play around as much as I like. The answer is just as my affairs fulfil some needs, my woman fulfils other needs. I love and need my woman. She is the mother of my children. She takes care of the house and me. I know if she ever had an affair I would kill her.

Life is a BITCH. You know what you are doing is wrong but you do it anyway. **Glenroy**

I am 26 years old. I am living with my girlfriend. We are not married. We may get married in the future. I work for a large chain of travel agencies. I said I might get married to my girlfriend because I had an affair with my girlfriend's sister.

I have been going out with my girlfriend for three or four years. I had an affair with her sister 10 months ago. The affair lasted about seven weeks. My girlfriend and her sister do not get on. They never have done.

Ever since I have known Murna, (my girlfriend's sister) she has flirted with me. At parties when we danced I felt her pressing herself on my leg. Once she even put my hand on her ass. I guest I encouraged her by not discouraging her.

My girlfriend went on holiday for ten days. At work there were special offers to Europe at very low prices. A group of us had arranged to travel together. I could not make it because at the last minute I was refused leave by my manager. My girlfriend and our friends went ahead without me. Otherwise they would have lost the opportunity of using the cheap tickets. Murna came to visit me on the second day. We talked. She left. We arranged to go to a club the following day.

After the club she came back to my house. We had a couple of drinks. Before I knew what was happening we were tearing each other's clothes off. We had a shower together. After the shower we went into my bedroom. She lied on her stomach legs wide apart. I notice for the first time how big her ass was. I compliment her on her ass. She invited me to kiss it. At first I refused. Then I accepted.

I kissed her ass, then I licked her bottom until I finally buried my tongue in her ass. She enjoyed it and asked me to finger her and finally we had anal sex.

We saw each other a few times after my girlfriend returned. We even made love on one occasion in the front room while my girlfriend slept upstairs.

The affair ended a few weeks after my girlfriend returned. I wish I could say I ended it, but I can't. Murna ended it. She said she had achieved what she wanted. I begged and begged Murna not to tell her sister. To my amazement she did not.

I had the affair because Murna was sexy and it turned me on at the time to have sex with my girlfriend's sister. What a fool I was. I should have been stronger.

Murna takes sadistic pleasure in knowing what she does. I live in total fear. I have come very close to telling my girlfriend. But how do you explain sleeping with her sister? I believe on an unconscious level that I have not made any plans to marry because I know my girlfriend's sister will eventually tell all.

I have this reoccurring nightmare. I am about to get married. The priest ask if there is anybody who knows of any lawful reason why this man and woman should not be married. At that point Murna jumps up and says, 'Yes, he slept with me. He is a no good lying, two timing, low down son of a bitch who deserves to rot in hell'. I always wake up at that point in a cold sweat.

It is becoming harder and harder to live with what I have done. I have made up my mind to tell my girlfriend what I have done. I have done the crime–it is about time I did the time. **Douglas**

I work for a very large company. I am in my late twenties and am engaged to my partner. We plan to get married once she has passed her professional exams and is working.

My dad was married to my mum for over 30 years before his death. They came to England in the late 1950s. I recently found out that my dad had an affair in the West Indies and got the woman involved pregnant. To my knowledge he was not unfaithful to my mum after they came to England. I am not too sure if this incident had any effect on my behaviour. I know I was angry when I found out I had a half sister that I had never met. We, as a family have never really discussed the matter.

I had a brief affair. I met Carol at a dinner party. We connected straight away. We talked all evening. At that time we never thought we would ever have an affair. I hardly saw my girlfriend who was busy studying. We had a non existent social life. When I needed her most she could not be found.

My dad was sick. Around the same time we got to know about my half-sister. The atmosphere became unbearable. The only person I knew I could turn to was not available. So I turned to Carol. At first we just talked. In fact I did all the talking. I was confused, angry at my dad and at the same time concerned because we knew he was seriously ill.

Carol helped me get through a very difficult time in my life. We got closer and closer. We made love on occasion, but that was not the reason for seeing her. I thought many times of leaving my girlfriend for Carol. She listened and cared about me. She appreciated me. In the end I did not continue to see Carol because I saw first-hand what an affair can do to innocent people.

Although I no longer see Carol, I often think of her. At times I feel she is the one I should be getting married to. I know I will see her again sooner or later.

I would like to say to the women reading this book that there are no magical answers to why men and women have affairs. For me it was because my partner was not available in my time of need. Even this is a cop-out because I knew where she was and what she was doing. You can interview a million men and women of all races and creeds and you will still not come up with a definitive and conclusive reason as to why people have affairs. A few common reasons may emerge, but not enough to make a generalisation.

The problem with affairs is that you should not have them in the first place. Once you have crossed that line it is hard to get back on the right track with your partner. The slightest excuse and you are back at it again. The best policy is not to have one in the first place.

Gary

Sometimes you just want to do the nasty. You want to fuck. You do not want to make love. I am 34. I have been with my partner for nearly nine years. Any man, irrespective of race, creed or colour, has affairs for one reason, sex. Men love sex. There could be all sorts of other reasons for having affairs, but I bet sex is top of the list or near the top. Men are driven by sex. I don't know why women have such a hard time understanding such a simple fact.

My woman is rather conservative. We have a normal sexual relationship. No kinky shit. No oral sex or S & M. The first time I had an affair I just drifted into it. I knew this black woman from the local sports centre. We played in the same squash league. The first time I met her we had a tremendous argument. She calls herself a 90s black woman. She was educated to degree level, she is very articulate, ambitious like hell, single, independent and does not want to be supported by any man.

The more I saw of her the more I liked her. One day I asked her out. We went out to dinner. We had an argument when it came to paying the bill. I wanted to pay. You would have thought it was an insult. She insisted on paying. I stuck to my guns. She only gave in because I agreed she would pay on the next date.

I was sexually attracted to Maureen. She was not a typical black woman, she did not sit around moaning about black men. She was funky; always looking for challenges, always daring you to go beyond the convention. She had the same attitude to sex. She tried everything at least once. That freaked me out.

The first time we had sex I came in her mouth. I cannot think of anything sexually I have not done with her. She is special. I must admit I wanted to leave my partner for her. Maureen, however, is too busy with her career. She is not interested in a long-term relationship. We still see each other. **Kevin**

I prefer not to tell you my name or anything personal about myself. But I will answer your question as to why I have had affairs. One reason I have affairs is because it helps my relationship with my woman. I tend to enjoy sex with her more after I have had sex with another woman. **Anonymous**

16 What can women do to prevent men having affairs?

"IF you loved me , you would not have done it".

"... But baby, I love you. I was thinking of you all the time I was with her. Look, it was nothing but a sex thing. It's not like what we have."

"Why did you do it? Was it something I did? If we had a problem, why didn't you come to me instead of going to her, Edwin?"

"I tried speaking to you several times; you just never listened. You always pretended everything was OK when you knew they it was not, Sandra".

" Did I miss something here? If people have problems, they don't try to fuck it away with some whore. They speak about it. They communicate. They don't go running to the first woman who is willing to listen."

"Sandra, a man can only take so much. You should have known something was wrong. Damn it woman we haven't made love for over a month. You use that thing between your legs like a weapon. 'If you are a good boy I will let you have some tonight'.

"What do you expect? I work all day, then you expect me to come home

and cook dinner, listen to you and the day you had at work. What about me? I am tired..."

"No, don't do anything you will regret Sandra. Put that knife down..."

Although our fictitious couple mentioned issues that contributed to the affair, in real life what can women do to prevent men having affairs? The answer according to men is... nothing. If a man respects his relationship he will not have an affair. It is really that simple.

When all is said and done there is not a great deal a woman can do to prevent her man from having an affair. If a man is determined to see someone else then he will irrespective of how well the woman treats him. I had a perfect relationship. We had no major rows, but I still had an affair. I honestly did not realise what I was doing was wrong until my partner found out and had a nervous breakdown. **Anonymous**

Whether a man has an affair or not depends for the most part on his character. Affairs come down to the integrity of the man, his sense of duty to his woman and his morals. If you really love someone, you do not show appreciation for that love by sleeping around -more so with the possibility of catching Aids or some other horrendous sexual disease. Men who have affairs for whatever reason should be brave enough to leave their relationship if they are not happy. **Lang**

Men who have affairs do so because they lack moral and spiritual guidance. They are controlled not by what is right but what they know is wrong. If you have an affair then there is a fundamental problem with you and/or your relationship. Do you think the majority of men who have affairs, would let their girlfriends or wives have affairs for the same reasons that they give their partners?

What if their loved one came up to them and said, "Can you forgive me, it was only a sex thang. That man you saw me with last night was only a friend. I stayed the night with him because he was having some trouble, you understand don't you?"

What about this excuse, "well we, you know, were, like, you know, having problems so I just thought I would fuck the shit out of this man. I am sure the problems we had before will now disappear. Don't you think so honey?"

How about this classic excuse often used by men? What if a black woman said to her black man: "Sugar, sweet pie, I had an affair because it's a woman thang. We women are brought up that way, you see it's nature, it's in our genes and shit. We cannot help but have affairs. It's a scientific fact we cannot stay with just one man. We were born to spread our sweetness." Any bets on how long the woman would survive?

Whatever reason a man may put forward for having an affair amounts to nothing more than an excuse. No man will accept their woman having an affair for the reasons men usually give, so why do they expect women to accept it? Affairs, to my mind, come down to the individual. If you love your partner you will know affairs are wrong and you are betraying someone's trust in you. If you do not know that then there is not much a woman can do to prevent you having an affair. **Shaun**

17 How would you find out if your partner is having an affair?

"I called your mother last night. She said she was not hospitalised. In fact she said she has never felt better. If you were not at the hospital with your mother, where have you been the last week, Claudia?"

"Did my mum really say that? She must have been joking, because I was with her this past week, I swear I was Leroy."

"Yeah, why would she lie, then?"

"To annoy you. Make you jealous. You know she does not like you."

"Well maybe. Why did you get so dressed up, wear all that perfume, if you were only going to the hospital? Are you having an affair?

"Yes I am. I cannot bear the secrecy any more. I am leaving you, Leroy. You are too damn stupid..."

Although it may hurt us to find out that our partners are having affairs, wouldn't it be great if we found out as easily as the fictitious character above?

I found out my girlfriend was having an affair by setting a trap for her. A few friends told me they saw her with some guy. I knew before they told me she was having an affair.

I told her my brother and I would be going out for the weekend. She believed me because my brother has a sound, and every now and again I go out with him. I had people watch the house. Late at night I had a call; the guy was in the house. I caught her and the guy in bed, my bed. We, my boys and I, beat the guy and checked him out naked. She is now history. **Trevor**

I worked for a communications company. It was easy for me to bug our phone. I listened into the conversation she was having with her lover. All I did was turn up at the place they were supposed to meet. To say she was surprised to see me is an understatement. **Wes**

I knew my girlfriend was having an affair. I knew because she did the same thing as I did when I once had an affair. She made mad passionate love to me. It was a change for her. Our love life was rather ordinary; all of a sudden she is trying new positions, doing all sorts of stuff we never did before, asking me to do and say things I never did before. She must have learned it from someone. **Anonymous**

If you suspect your partner is having an affair, then I suppose you can do the stupid thing and ask her. What if she lies and says no? What then? What I did was hire a detective. He got me pictures of them together. I posted one of the pictures to my ex and waited to see her reaction. When she opened the envelope it was one of the best and worst days of my life. **Anonymous**

I found out my ex was having an affair when she fucking told me. Bitch. **Anonymous**

If she is not interested in sex, or if she is always tired. The 'I have a headache syndrome', you know something is wrong. The opposite is also true; if she is keen to have sex but you can tell the desire is not there. She may be covering up–having sex so that you will not suspect anything. **Anonymous**

It is easy to tell if your partner (man or woman) is having an affair. They give signals and in some cases may even tell you. They will tell you in a manner which may suggest they are joking. Make no mistake, they are serious. Often the guilt make them confess. If you can recognise the signs then you can tell whether your partner is having an affair. From experience the signs to look out for are:

- Sudden withdrawal from sex for no apparent reason.
- Drastic change in routine. For instance, going out alone more or with friends.
- Best friends suddenly call more, and invite your partner out more than usual.
- Their attitude towards you changes. It can be for the better or worse. Again for no obvious reason.
- Love bites on the neck, men are very inventive at making up excuses to cover up love bites.
- Women will notice when they have sex with their boyfriend that when they come there is not much semen. If you have not had sex with your partner very recently this could mean one of two things. Either he released through masturbation. Or he released into someone else. That is how my ex-girlfriend found out. She had her suspicions before. When we had sex and I did not release anything she just knew. I wanted out of the relationship so I admitted it.
- Inconsistent excuses. She is dressed in her best outfit but insists she is not going anywhere special. Or she wears expensive perfume when she is going to visit friends.

There are also obvious signs like the phones being hang up when you answer. Or if you are next to your partner when it rings she gives one word replies and hurries to get off the phone. **Franklin**

I found out my girlfriend was having an affair when I caught her giving head to a guy in a car. It was one of those inexplicable freak accidents. I was driving home- I cannot remember from where-when I thought I saw her car on a side road. Out of curiosity I drove up to the car and there they were. All hell broke loose. **Anonymous**

I don't know how I would find out if my partner was having an affair. I know how my partner found out I was having an affair. Her friend told her. I went half-way across the country. I booked a hotel in the 'whitest' town I could find. I thought no one could possible find out. I went to an all-white area because my partner and I did not have any white friends we mixed with socially.

I thought the only black people would be myself and the black woman I was having the affair with. I almost died from fucking shock seeing my girlfriend's friend behind the reception desk. I believe she was there training or something. To this day I am not certain why she was there and on that day. **Anonymous**

My girlfriend came home early and found me in bed with her best friend. Otherwise she would never have found out. To this day I believe it was her best friend who told her to come home early. I believe the stupid girl told my girlfriend because she wanted me to herself. I left them both. It was perfect because I was seeing someone else, who I wanted to be with. Being found out was perfect because it killed two birds with one stone. **Anonymous**

PART THREE

Brothers on love and sex

18 What makes a woman a good lover?

WHAT qualities must one possess in order to be elevated into the 'good lover' category? It is impossible for every woman to have all the qualities listed by men in the following pages. However, they give a good indication as to what men think makes a good lover. You may not always agree with what is said. You may have your own ideas.

Open-mindedness

A woman who is open-minded and willing to experiment is more often than not a very good lover. This type of woman is adventurous and does not always stick to boring convention. **LH**

Judging from experience, the women I have found are good, and who kept me coming back for more, were the women who were open-minded and willing to experiment. I love this type of woman because she knows that often men are just as stuck for ideas on what they should do as women are. **Anonymous**

Women who are prone to experiment are at times the best lovers because they are willing to challenge their sexual inhibitions. **FE**

Women who are open-minded and willing to experiment are good lovers because they have a flexible approach to sex. They try new and varied positions and are always seeking new ways to enhance their sexual pleasure. **PY**

Taking the initiate

There is nothing better than a woman who initiates sex. I get all excited thinking about it. If a woman wants to surprise her partner and wants to be considered a good lover all she has to do is initiate sex. Men, I know for a fact, get tired of always being the ones to initiate sex. I have been in situations where I know my partner wanted to make love, but because I did not initiate it nothing happened and she went to bed frustrated.

Some of the best sex I have had was when my long-term girlfriend made the first move. I felt wanted and turned on that she wanted me. That thought made me love her harder. Also, if women initiate sex it makes love-making a two-way thing. You don't always have to make love because the man wants to. **Randolph**

Acting out fantasies

Not all fantasies are safe, or even desirable, to act out. There are, however, a few that are harmless. I have found that if a woman is willing to act out your and her fantasies that makes love making all the more enjoyable, and the woman all the more appealing. My fantasy was to have my girlfriend swallow my semen. In my desire to 'protect' her, I never told her my fantasy, that is until we talked about fantasies and I shared my fantasy. Now and again, as a treat, we act out each others fantasy. **Anonymous**

Patience

The truth of the matter is that men do not always know what they are suppose to do in bed. We are not all super-studs. Even the men who consider themselves good lovers must have learnt their skills. You do not get up one morning and find you are a great lover capable of pleasing women. A woman who understands this and is patient I find is a good lover. **HT**

Patience in a woman often translates to her being a good lover. A patient lover is not going to make demands you cannot possibly fulfil.She will not put you under unnecessary pressure. She will be wise enough to know haste makes waste. **Eddie**

Confidence in their sexuality

Women who know they are sexy from within and have confidence make very good lovers. I have been out with dope women who were useless in bed-because they did not have any confidence in themselves. **FG**

Women who believe in themselves usually make good lovers. If a woman knows she is beautiful from within; that inner quality will come out in her actions in bed. She will not be self-conscious, she will not want to hide her body, or think a man is with her because he is doing her a favour. Her attitude is 'you have to appreciate me, and yes you better believe I am fine'. That attitude usually makes for a good lover. **Jeff**

Women who are secure in themselves and confident make good lovers. They are usually bold in bed, and make love in daylight not just in the dark. They wear anything in bed irrespective of their size. They make no apologies for who they are, what they expect in bed and what they are about to do to you sexually. Women with these qualities never fail in bed. **Emmanuel**

Stamina

I am a very fit individual. I tend to rate women great lovers or average lovers depending on how much stamina they have. I do not make love for hours, but I do go on for a very long time. **TE**

A woman who can keep up and want it for a long time, one who is interested in quality and quantity does it for me every time. **VO**

Enjoyment of sex

A woman who enjoys sex is more often than not a good lover. It stands to reason that you are not going to be good unless you enjoy what you are doing. **Anonymous**

A woman who enjoys sex is a good lover. If she enjoys sex she makes that extra effort. She wants it as much as you do. You both look forward to making love. **Anonymous**

Good Communication

The only way to find out what each other likes or dislikes is to tell each other. Couples often put up with a dull and repetitive sexual routine because they are afraid to say exactly what they like and what they dislike. A good lover is going to talk to her partner telling him what she likes. **Anonymous**

19 What makes a woman a bad lover?

WE use our own sexual experience to judge what sort of person constitutes a bad lover. Therefore, any list of what constitutes a bad lover will be subjective and a mirror of personal experience. For example, you may think a woman who stays in the same position is a bad or boring lover; a man who is content to make love in that one position may think his partner is a terrific lover.

Several respondents made the point that women and men are never bad lovers. Each person does what they know best up to that point in their lives.

Dislike of sex

I have yet to find a bigger turn-off that a woman who acts like she does not like sex. The quickest way to get rid of a man is to act like you do not like sex. He would avoid you like a leper. **Anonymous**

I hate women who act like they do not like sex. These women make derogatory remarks about sex, act all shy and embarrassed when someone is talking about sex. They are uncomfortable about their partners expressing their sexuality, they never enjoy sex because they see it as something they have to endure. These women make bad lovers because they make men feel ashamed of wanting sex. After trying to make love to these women you feel guilty, like you did something wrong or dirty. **Michael**

Giving too many directions

A woman can be a good lover, but nothing turns men off more than a woman that gives too many directions. She would say, 'oh baby do this, oh baby please do that again, oh honey do it like you did last week, no do it this way'. On and on she goes without stopping. If you can get away with faking an orgasm you would do it. **Isaiah**

Passivity

A woman who never participates or shows any sign of movement is a terrible lover. All she does is lie back and think of king and country. She adopts one position and stays there for the duration. She will not move come hell or high water. Sometimes you have to pinch her to see if she is still alive. **Winston**

Being afraid to touch

Women who never, ever touch or explore a man's body often make bad lovers. Making love is a two-way thing, if the woman does not explore her partner's body it makes for a very uneventful evening.

Women are happy for you to enter them, but are not willing to touch your prick, that is very annoying and insulting. It makes me feel like there is something wrong with me. You are prepared to let me enter you, but you are not prepared to touch me. I rate such women bad lovers. I like women to touch me all over. There is nothing worse than a woman who makes no attempt to touch your penis, not even during foreplay. **PT**

Selfishness

She thinks only about herself. She will only try something new if it brings her more pleasure. She will never try something or do something because you like it. There is no give and take. Only take on her part.

A selfish lover cares only about her gratification. I have been out with these women. Their attitude is; 'I got mine, you get yours'. The problem is they never let you get yours because as soon as they are finished, they switch off and sex has effectively finished. I went out with a woman several years ago who wanted me to go down on her but she felt she could not possibly degrade herself by doing the same to me. **Anonymous**

Self-consciousness

A woman may have the potential to be a great lover. What lets her down is that she is ashamed of her body, which means she is always covering up and hiding under the blankets. She has no self-confidence. She fails because she expects to fail. Often self-conscious women are inhibited, unwilling to break away from convention. **Anonymous**

Faking it

Fakers often make bad lovers. The contradictory thing is that they think they are good because they can fake an orgasm. I once made love to a woman who started to scream and shout before I had done anything. I had to tell her I appreciated the compliment but shouldn't she wait 'till I at least put the damn thing in. **FD**

20 What is your favourite sexual position and where is the best place for making love?

MORE than 40 per cent of the men who took part in the study said their favourite sexual position was the missionary position. However, many noted that new sexual positions are discovered all the time. Many also said that although sex usually started off in the missionary position it rarely ended there. As one respondent noted.

" I would say the missionary position is my favourite. Mind you, we are quite relaxed about sex and do whatever feels natural at the time. My girlfriend once tried a new position; it was so painful that I thought my dick had broken in several places. It was very embarrassing going to the doctor and trying to explain what happened. We never tried that position again."
Anonymous

My favourite position is the missionary position. I get pleasure in watching my partner enjoy herself. The position is very personal. It is a wonderful position. I notice I last a lot longer than in other positions. **Anonymous**

I like the missionary position because it is the most natural of positions. It is not an elaborate position, nor is it exotic. I believe it is the position in which you get the closest to your partner. You can hear each other's heart beat. **Anonymous**

The missionary position is my favourite position. It is also the position where I seem to have the least control. **Paul**

Woman on top is my favourite position. It is one of the few positions where you can lie back and relax. In that position the woman is doing most of the work. You can take in the view of the woman working and appreciate what a lovely woman she is. With the woman on top you can also appreciate what a wonderful and joyous thing sex is. **CC**

With the woman on top you are in a way passive. She has the dominant role, she is doing all the fucking. All you have to do is keep it up. I like it in that position when the woman pins your hands down and pump's even harder. I also like that position because the woman can suck your nipples. **Mac**

Variations of the doggy style are my favourite positions. If the woman I am dating has a beautiful ass then I love to do it doggy style. The thought of that ass bouncing off my body is a real turn-on. **Anonymous**

Standing or leaning against the wall are my two favoured positions. I like these positions because their is a rawness and a primitive quality to them. **Dennis**

I like the position where the woman has her legs over my shoulder. I can go really deep. **Lenroy**

My favourite position is where the woman is on her back with her legs held back and I am on top. **VC**

My favourite position involves my partner on her back with both of her legs astride my shoulder. **BU**

My favourite position is 69. I have not got to tell you how oral sex is taboo in the black community. It is very rare to get black men talking openly about oral sex or admitting that they do it. Nevertheless I like it–doing it and receiving it. Apart from 69, I like the position where my girlfriend kneels over my face and I eat her. An alternative is where I kneel and she sucks me till I am about to come. **Anonymous**

My favourite position depends on what part of the woman's body I like. Men, on the whole, are either ass men, leg men, breast men, pum pum men etc. I am an ass man. So I tend to favour positions that show off the woman's ass. My friend is a legs man. He tends to favour positions where the woman can wrap her long legs around him. **Daniel**

Black people can dance, more so our women. My favourite position starts with me dancing a slow tune with my woman against the wall. I slowly get rid of her clothes. I pin her against the wall and enter her. Sometimes she does a go-go dance to get me in the mood. After she shakes her waist twice I am frothing at the mouth. We experiment to see what position we can get into while she is still dancing.

Dance is so sensuous that it makes sense to add it to the love-making process occasionally. If both of you are willing and do not feel shy you should try it. **AA**

I have not got a favourite position. I am still exploring. **Anonymous**

The best place to make love

MORE than 90 per cent of the men I interviewed or who completed my questionnaire said the bedroom was the most likely place they would make love.

One of the reasons given was that the bedroom has the least chance of couples being interrupted. Another reason is simply because of the amount of time spent in the bedroom. Couples spend more time in that room than any other. A third reason given is that is is the natural place to make love. Other places were seen as being more adventurous and exotic, for example, the kitchen table or the staircase.

The final reason given was that the longer you have been together the less spontaneous you are likely to be as a couple. Love-making becomes more routine

and planned, which means you are more likely to make love in the bedroom.

I love to make love in the bath or in the shower. It is a great place to make love. Water and soap can be so sexy. **Kelvin**

I love to make love in open spaces-for example, in my car. We find a deserted or quiet spot and make love. The change in scenery and the added danger enhances the excitement. **Donald**

If you want to be daring, make love in a forest. It gives you an extra buzz. It is nice to make love in a natural, safe environment. Too many couples do not take the risk. **LA**

I once knew this woman who for some reason I always wanted to seduce and make love to her on the staircase. I can tell you the experience was just as good as I had imagined. I love making love on staircases. It's romantic and different. **Bradley**

Once I made love to my partner on our friend's carpet in the bathroom. I believe I had one of my hardest erections ever. Since that time we always make it a point to fuck when we go out to parties. Once we even tried a club, at the back of the speakers. It is a challenge that both of us enjoy. It is a break from the norm. It does not happen often, but when it does we both enjoy the experience. **Anonymous**

I am from the West Indies. Back home we have lovers' lanes where couples make out in their cars. You can even make out on the beach. Fucking on the beach, however, is not very romantic, especially for women. They discover sand weeks after the event. As a result of my experiences back home I tend to favour open spaces. There are one or two deserted spots where you can make out without being caught. **Anonymous**

I am like Martini. I like to make love anywhere, any place and any time. Once it feels right for both of us we do it. **Philip**

21 What is the most embarrassing thing that has happened to you sexually?

ONE of the respondents said that it is impossible for anyone who makes love not to have at least one embarrassing moment. Anything from the first time when you did not know what you were doing or supposed to do, to not being able to rise to the occasion. I tend to agree.

Prostitutes

My wife went off sex completely after our third child. I managed to go without making love for a number of years. One day we had an argument and I went to a prostitute. I wore a condom. That is the most embarrassing thing I have done sexually. That was two years ago. I love my wife dearly and will never forgive myself. I often try to tell her. **Anonymous**

I was young. I thought I would never lose my virginity. Everyone I knew seemed to be talking about sex. Everyone was doing it but me. The feeling is similar to when you buy a new car. You never noticed the car on the road before, but once you have bought that car you suddenly notice the car everywhere. Well, I wanted to have sex. I suddenly noticed that everyone I knew was having sex. I suddenly notice how much it was on TV, in magazines and films. I did not have a girlfriend at the time. So I went with a prostitute. I believe that was my most embarrassing and shameful sexual experience. It is something that will haunt me for the rest of my life. **Anonymous**

I tried going with a prostitute once. She took my money and said that I should meet her in some house. I never saw her again or my money. I was conned. Although I was embarrassed at losing the money, I was also happy because I did not go with her. **DE**

The first time

The most embarrassing thing that happened to me was telling this older woman I was an experienced lover when in fact I was a virgin. I was clumsy and nervous. The whole night was a disaster. **Anonymous**

I remember on my first attempt at making love I asked the girl what hole was I supposed to put it in. I believe that was my most embarrassing sexual experience. **Anonymous**

Not many men have not had an embarrassing moment on their first sexual encounter with a woman. On your own you can cope. All you need is privacy and a great imagination. The first time you make love is different. You are afraid, clumsy and apologetic.

My first attempt at making love was a disaster. Everything that could have gone wrong did. I did not know how to put on a condom. I bit her tits too hard rather than sucking them. The condom was too big. My erection was too soft. I came too soon. My brother came home earlier than expected. The whole night was an embarrassment and disaster. **OT**

To beg or not to beg?

I suppose the most embarrassing thing I have done sexually is beg for sex. At the time I knew it was wrong. I knew the next day I would feel bad. I also knew I just had to get some of her sweet potato pie.

I was seeing this woman from work. I went to see her one weekend. In short, we began to talk about things we would never do sexually. I cannot remember what she said she would never do. I told her I would never beg for sex. I went as far as saying people who do are pathetic. That was her cue. She went upstairs and changed. She came back downstairs wearing the most alluring and sexy body suit.

She put on some music and danced the way only black women know how to dance. She teased me saying if I want some I will have to beg. I resisted. I wanted to beg. I resisted. I watched her breasts. The thigh-high leather boots. The thong under the body suit. I dropped down on my knees and begged. I begged like I have never begged before. On a more serious note, the relationship did not last long after that incident. Every time I saw her I could not get what I did out of my mind. **Anonymous**

The most embarrassing thing I have done is beg for sex. It gives my partner power over me, which she seems to like. A man will do next to anything for sex. The shame and embarrassment is not till the act has finished. Then you ask yourself "Did I really do that? **Anonymous**

Smell

I once met this woman at a friend's party. We exchanged numbers and eventually we met up. I went down low. I swear this woman had probably never washed because I have never smelt anything so bad in my entire life. I was physically sick. **WD**

The most embarrassing thing is not bathing before going down on a hot summer's day. **Jonathan**

Quick

I was with this woman and I guess the first time I came literally within seconds. I made an excuse saying I really wanted her, I was too excited, but that the second time would be better. After a long break, we tried again. The same thing happened. Maybe faster than the first time. **HT**

There is nothing more embarrassing than a woman telling you, 'Is that it?' and you know it is because you just broke the 100-metres record. The only problem is that you were not running the 100 metres. It took me much longer to put on a condom than to make love with an ex-girlfriend. She was not amused and was not afraid to tell me. That in itself I could live with. But she told her friends. That was embarrassing. **BJM**

I like foreplay like the next man or woman. On one occasion I got so carried away that I came. A few seconds later the woman asked me if I was ready for the main course. It was really embarrassing telling her I already had it. **Femi**

All rise

The most embarrassing moment was being so drunk that I could not make love to my partner. The harder I tried the worse the problem got. I just could not get an erection. That was the most embarrassing thing that ever happened to me sexually. **JS**

I once pursued a woman for eight months. I told her how I would play with her body like Miles Davis plays his instrument-you know, professional, long, strong and with plenty of improvisation. Eventually she relented. On that particular night I was not up to it. For what ever reason, Junior (that is what I call my penis) would not rise. That was embarrassing. **Anonymous**

Someone is coming

I was caught by my mum making love to this woman in the front room. That was embarrassing. **Dean**

I was caught by my sister, making out with her best friend. That was embarrassing to all those concerned. **Anonymous**

The most embarrassing sexual experience did not happen to me, it happened to my dad. I was sent home from school and I caught him in bed with my mum's friend. **Anonymous**

I was caught by my ex-girlfriend's Dad in her bedroom. He came in without knocking. He went out without saying a word, so naturally I carried on. I was too close to coming to stop. A few seconds later he came back with a fucking sword. I grabbed my trousers and jumped out of the window. I did not stop running. I have never been back. **Jason**

Size

The most embarrassing thing that has happened to me was when an ex-partner said 'I cannot feel it'. It was embarrassing because she was a new girlfriend and I knew that this was the best and biggest my erection was going to get. **IVC**

I have never forgotten my most embarrassing moment. It took absolutely ages to get over it. I was about to get into bed with a new partner and she said, 'oh look yours is not as big as my last boyfriend's. I thought all men were the same size'. Up till that moment I had never really thought about size. **HF**

A very wicked lady friend once said to me 'put it in then'. I already had. **Anonymous**

Once when I was fully erect and proud of my erection my ex-girlfriend said, 'no don't be silly size really does not matter'. **RN**

Speaking out

The worst thing a woman has said to me in bed is, 'haven't you finished yet? Please come quickly I am tired'. Definitely a passion-killer. What else can you do after she has said that to you. What I did was get dressed and left. I have never seen her since. For a woman to say that to a man can mean only one of three things. Firstly, she is extremely insensitive. Secondly, she is really tired or thirdly she does not care for you or what you are doing to her. I left because we had been having trouble for almost a year. I suppose we both knew the relationship was over. **Rupert**

The worst thing a woman has said to me in bed is that she used to be a man. Followed by, 'just get on with it'. The only thing I got on with is almost killing him. **DJ**

You cannot please all the people all the time. But for me and a lot of other men the most embarrassing thing a woman can say is that you are no good in bed. Chances are you will either never have sex again or treat it like falling off a bike. You know get up and get right back on. The only problem is that when you have fallen off a bike too often you think maybe this is not for you. **SP**

My most embarrassing moment was when a woman who I wanted for a very long time said I only did it because I felt sorry for you. **Larry**

An ex-partner once told me I only did it to show you what you were missing and what you will be missing. I am not too sure whether it fits the most embarrassing moment criterion. **Keith**

My most embarrassing moment was when my ex-girlfriend called me by someone else's name. To add insult to injury, I knew the guy. That was embarrassing. **QT**

A woman I was dating at the time called me by my brother's name when we were making love. The old slut. That was embarrassing for me, but painful for her and my brother. **Anonymous**

We are not all super-studs. The worst and most embarrassing thing a woman can say to you is you are no good in bed. Or as in my case, and I quote verbatim: "Boy you can't fuck. Don't waste my time again." **Anonymous**

S & M

An ex-girlfriend got her revenge by handcuffing me to the four pillars of the bed thus leaving me to be discovered by my wife. **Anonymous**

I know why black people do not partake in sadomasochism-it fucking hurts. The first and last time I indulged in S&M I cried like a baby. Real tears. This woman hit me with a real fucking whip. I thought I was Toby, from Roots. Boy, that was embarrassing. **Anonymous**

I once went out with a woman (not black) who was into all sorts of freaky shit. She had me bark like a dog. Mind you I drew the line when she wanted me to shit on her. That would have been embarrassing. **Anonymous**

22 Are you more or less likely to respect a woman if you have sex on your first date?

FEW questions elicited such diverse responses as this one. Everyone has a viewpoint on sex on the first date. No two individuals will agree on how long you should wait before going to bed.

The contradictory attitude of society does not help. On the one hand men are congratulated if they are successful on the first night. Women, on the other hand, are viewed as loose, deviant or lacking in morals for sleeping with a man on the first date.

The majority of black men-60 per cent, said they are less likely to respect a woman they have slept with on the first date. Thirty per cent said it would make no difference and 10 per cent said they are more likely to respect a woman who slept with them on the first date.

Less likely to respect (60 per cent)

No one respects anything that comes too easily. Sex on the first meeting is too easy. I would never, ever go to bed with a woman on the first date, not with Aids so rampant. If she gives it up that easily it could not be that good. She cannot possibly have any sort of respect for herself. **Leroy**

Any woman who goes to bed with a man on the first date is asking for trouble. Chances are the man will not respect her in the morning. When It has happened with me I have always wondered if she has done it before with some other guy. In the woman's defence, I suppose if she does have sex with a man on the first date then it was probably a sex thing for her too. **Brian**

Generally the man's view is that if she had sex with me on the first date then she must have been desperate for sex. Therefore I cannot see how you can respect a woman who has sex on the first date. **Anonymous**

A woman who goes to bed with a man on the first date runs the risk that he will not respect her afterwards. On reflection, although I actively pursued sex on the first date, I must admit I tended not to have a high regard for the women who gave in to my advances. My advice to women is, if you want more than a sexual relationship, do not have sex on the first date. **Dean**

The only thing I can say in relation to sex on the first date is this. Men rate women depending on how long it takes to get them into bed. They give themselves extra point for having sex on the first date. What are the chances of a man respecting a woman he has sex with on the first date? My guess is that the chances are slim to none. **BU**

It makes no difference (30 per cent)

A lot of hypocrisy surrounds the issue of sex on the first date.

Women say they never do it. If men are doing it, who are they doing it with! It makes no difference to me if I have sex with a woman on the first date or the tenth. You have to judge a person for who and what they are. You cannot, in this day and age, come to a conclusion about someone because you slept with them on the first date. **FE**

My question is, when is it ok for a woman to go to bed with a man? Are the men and women who object to having sex on the first date, more comfortable waiting until the second date. What about the third or forth date? If you still find that objectionable, what about the second month or fifth month? what about waiting until you get to know him, which in reality can take a lifetime.

The truth of the matter is you cannot please all of the people all of the time. Someone, somewhere will object whether you wait a day or a year. My advice is to do whatever you think you can live with. To hell with what people say. **Peter**

Women in the past, and to a lesser extent today, have been brought up to believe in no sex before marriage, or outside a 'caring' relationship. Therefore, the notion of sex on the first date horrifies many women. In a male-dominated society it is in man's interest to keep women from accepting the idea of casual sex. Before the spread of Aids nobody ever tried to discourage men from having casual sex. In all honesty I would not respect a woman any less because we had sex on our first date.**CC**

More likely to (10 per cent)

Sex on the first date is one of those issues where people feel cool saying they do not do it. It is also one of those issues where it is easy to take the moral high ground and condemn it along with the people who do it. That is why I tend to have a high respect for women (men have openly pursued sex on the first date ever since they discovered the main function of their dick) who are not afraid to have sex when they want, whether it is the first or the 1000th date. **Anonymous**

I am a 37-year-old divorced man. I don't want a relationship with every woman I meet. I believe women should have sex on the first date if that is what they want to do and not be made to feel guilty. **Anonymous**

Sex between two consenting adults is no one's business. If a woman sleeps with you on the first date it does not necessarily means she is lacking in morals. **BB**

Who has time to wait for sex? People should have sex as and when they please, as long as you take the necessary precautions. My respect for a woman will not lessen because we sleep together on the first meeting. I am just grateful I did not have to wait for it. **AE**

23 Should you have sex with your ex?

"Long time no see Tarmera. How you keeping?"

"I am very well Kenneth. How long has it been since we broke up?

" What? You don't know, Tarmera?"

"Well, in actual fact we were last together two years, three months, one week and 24 minutes ago..."

"Who is counting then? Tarmera, you look great; in fact, you look fine."

"You look all that yourself. Why did you call me over to your house when we have not seen each other for so long?"

"Well Tarmera, I missed you. I was thinking about you, what we had. And-I don't know-I thought, we might, you know..."

"Are you crazy? I think I know what you are getting at. I have been in your house less than an hour and you are hitting on me Kenneth. What! Do you now see me as a bit of fluff? Have you no respect for me or what we had?"

"I respect you and I respect what we had even more. It's just that you have been on my mind for the past three months Tarmera. I finally got the courage to call you today. So I thought I would make the most of it–prepare you dinner. Have wine and then who knows...?"

"Since you put it that way maybe I can stay. I would hate for you to waste all that food.

I hope you prepared breakfast. In fact, since you want to see me so much, when do I get to move in? I can"t wait for us to start all over again..."

OUR fictitious couple had not seen each other for over two years. However, the possibility for misunderstanding was very clear. In real life, according to the men who answered this question, having sex with your ex gives way to all sorts of misunderstandings. For example, does the fact that you slept with each other mean you still care for each other? Was it simply a sexual thing between two people who were once physically attracted to each other? Was it only for old time's sake? Is it a sign of things to come?

Not a good idea (85 per cent)

Sex with your ex is not a good idea. The problem is that you do not find out it is a bad idea until you have done the deed and gone to bed with her. Women are often brought up to equate sex with love. I have found that any time I have had sex with an ex-girlfriend she assumes I want her back. **Anonymous**

Sex complicates matters. You may get back together, from that initial encounter, only to discover that the problems you broke up over are still there and have not been dealt with. The mistake I made was to have sex with my ex. We got back together only to break up eight months later for the same reason as before. I will never have sex with an ex again. **NHG**

Anyone, a man or woman, who is thinking of having sex with their ex, should ask themselves these simple questions: Is sleeping with your ex going to make you feel good or benefit you in any way? What are your real motives for sleeping with your ex? Is it just for sex or do you expect something to happen as a result?

The answers to these questions should give you a very good idea as to whether you should sleep with your ex. I wish I had the knowledge I have now. I made the mistake of sleeping with my ex. She thought I wanted to get back together. It caused her so much pain when she found out differently. **Chuck**

The overwhelming majority of men said it was a bad idea to sleep with your ex. The following views are those of the minority of men who said it was a good idea to sleep with an ex-partner. These men often had hidden agendas; it was never as plain as simply sleeping with their ex.

A good idea (15 per cent)

It is a good idea to sleep with your ex. It is the very best way I know of getting revenge for her leaving you. **Anonymous**

Sleeping with my ex is an ego thing. You know the saying 'twice as nice the second time round'. With an ex I see it as a challenge. Can you get this woman, who you once slept with, to go to bed with you again? **Donald**

If both of you do not intend to get back together and you understand that it is just a sex thing, then I would have to say sex with your ex is a good thing. **Jr**

Sex with your ex is good. For the past year I have been having sex with my ex. As far as she is concerned we are back together. As far as I am concerned I am just having sex with a woman I use to go out with. In my mind I know I don't want to have a relationship with this woman. But as long as the sex is good I am prepared to let her think what she wants. **Anonymous**

Sex with your ex is good as it is the only way to find out if you want your ex. If at the end you just want to go home and forget about her, then you know you should not get back together. **Mark**

Are you joking? Sex with your ex is a great idea. Bwoy, when ting them tuff, and you have no woman who else is there for sex other than your ex? You get some, go home, have a good sleep, then return next time for more. Perfect. **Anonymous**

24 What is your greatest sexual fear?

Impotence

If men answer this question honestly, they will admit their number one fear is impotence. We are all aware of Aids. I believe if you sit any brother down and give him a choice between catching Aids and being impotent, the brother is going to choose life and be impotent. The problem is that no one is ever presented with a clear-cut decision like this. So that is why I know brother's number one fear is being impotent. **Anonymous**

I know of the existence of Aids. But my greatest sexual fear is being impotent. A man has to do what he has to do. A man cannot live by bread alone, if you know what I mean. **TG**

My greatest sexual fear is being impotent. Getting a sexually transmitted disease is always at the back of your mind. But you can minimise the risk by practising safe sex and being monogamous. I would rather be dead than impotent. I suppose one good thing about being impotent is that you cannot get any diseases. **Anonymous**

Social disease

I am a young man who wishes to marry and eventually have a family. Therefore anything that stops me achieving that is my greatest fear. At the moment I would say getting a sexually transmitted disease (STD) is at the top of my list. **Anonymous**

I love sex, but not enough to die for it. The thought of catching a STD scares the shit out of me.

I love you to death. This statement is literally true if your ass gets Aids. My sexual fear is getting something I cannot get a jab for. **Anonymous**

Premature ejaculation

Men are sexual animals; anything that takes away the ability to enjoy sex is going to be viewed as a threat. I suppose I have got my worst nightmare. I suffer from premature ejaculation. It has made my life hell. I have tried all sorts of cures, taken potions and remedies from back home, all to no avail. The only difference in my mind between premature ejaculation and STD is that one kills you physically and the other kills you mentally. I have been faster than Superman for a long time; premature ejaculation has ruined my life. I lost my girlfriend, and because of the embarrassment of premature ejaculation I have made the decision not to have any more relationships. Unless you suffer from this you can never know how it feels. **Anonymous**

Other

Loosing interest with age is one of my sexual fears. I am at that age where you no longer fuck. You now make love to your partner. I worry whether I will lose interest the older I get. It is a subject I keep meaning to ask older couples. I find the subject so personal that I haven't found the courage to ask anyone. **Paul**

I cannot imagine not making love or not wanting to make love to my wife. I have been told that the older you get the less likely you are to have sex. That scares me. I cannot imagine sitting back and saying to young people: ' I remember when I use to do that. I was good too'. **Winston**

The stereotype is that old people do not do 'it'. My fear is that one day I will get up and suddenly sex will no longer be part of my life. **PD**

An old black man once told me a joke. He asked us, whether we knew why black men hold their penis. The answer, he said, is because the white man has taken everything else so we are just making sure it is still there. Losing my sexual organ is one of my greatest fears. I keep having this dream that someone steals my penis. In my dream I get up to go to the toilet and there is nothing there. Its gone. I cannot tell you how relieved I am in the morning when I realise it was only a dream. **Anonymous**

I often think of Bobbit. He is the man who had his piece cut off by his wife. I often think of what would have happened if they had not found it. I suppose it is not worth thinking about. My greatest fear is one of my women getting the same idea as Bobbit's wife and cutting my piece. **Anonymous**

25 What is the best chat-up line you have used or heard?

COMEDIANS often say the secret of comedy is timing. If you have not got timing then your gag or joke will not work. It would appear that the same applies to chat-up lines. To be effective the timing must be right. Chat-up lines are also problematic. For instance, a chat-up line that works in one situation will not necessarily work in another. The other problem is that they are often throw-away lines. According to the men interviewed it is not advisable to use a chat-up line more than once.

Chat-up lines must also appear authentic; nothing is worst than a chat-up line that comes across as exactly that. Women don't usually respond to them according to the men who use them. Finally, chat-up lines only get your foot in the door. They break the ice. It is up to you to persuade the woman that you are worth talking to.

The best chat-up line I have used or heard is this one: You ask a young lady, 'does it hurt?' as though concerned. Her response, more than likely, will be, 'does what hurt?' You say 'the fall from heaven'. **Anonymous**

My best chat-up line is to have no chat-up line. To be successful you have to be sharp. You have to react to the situation. I was at a club recently. This very attractive woman who was standing next to me had just turned this guy away. So I turned to her and said, 'Don't you just hate it when that happens?' She laughed and said yes. Before long we got talking and I got to dance with her all night. **Zakery**

Listen to records if you are stuck for chat-up lines. The older the record the better. Never ever claim it as your own. If the woman knows the record admit it and tell her you were stuck for words, but the record lyrics were exactly what you wanted to express to her. Tell her that if you could sing the song you would have done so. **GY**

The best chat-up line I have heard is this one: Don't tell me your last name because it is going to be mine'. The guy who said it was a player. The line was successful because he was in a singles bar. **Richard**

The fact of the matter is chat-up lines do not always work on women. Compliments have a far greater chance of success in my experience. Compliment anything, from the dress to the shoes. Even tell her the 24 carat gold ring in her nose really suits her. **Anonymous**

If I could eat you I would eat you a thousand times. **Anonymous**

Tonight may be the last time I see you, I just had to take the chance and introduce myself. **Over heard**

"Chances are you are either married, engaged, a lesbian, recovering from a bad relationship, single or a hater of men. Which one is it?" Mind you, with this line if she does not like you you are giving her the opportunity to brush you off by saying she is married or a lesbian. **Anonymous**

I just had to take the chance and introduce myself to you because I would like to get to know you. **YT**

I believe we must all pay a price for what we want. I would rather you reject me right now than to go home and say 'if only'. **Cee**

Lady you look so fine you make the other women in this place jealous. **Overheard**

You look the way Billy Holiday sings, cool and classy. **Anonymous**

You know you remind me of my mum, you have the same smile as her. **LB**

I did not believe in angels until I saw you. I hope you don't get your wings and fly away. How you doing? **Anonymous**

You look nice, just like my mum's Sunday dinner. **Rodders**

I know it is somewhat presumptuous of me, but I would like to see the sunrise with you. **NB**

Me and you were made to at least get to know each other. Take a chance: lets talk. What is your name? **AA**

How does it feel to be the best-looking woman here? **Anonymous**

Take it from me, you do not need any silly chat-up lines to be successful with women. All you need to know are two words, 'hi', and 'thank you', well maybe three words. Take it from the Don, all you have to do is go up to any woman and say 'hi'. If she speaks to you or rejects your advances, say 'thank you' and move on to the next woman. **Anonymous**

26 What is the worst chat-up line you have used or heard?

THE men who responded reported the greatest failure with unimaginative chat-up lines and over- familiar ones.

Haven't I seen you before? **Anonymous**

Don't I know you from somewhere? **HU**

You look familiar. Have you ever been to... The man will then produce a long list of countries or local areas or certain fictitious names. **Anonymous**

What is a girl like you doing in a nice place like this? Or what is a girl like you doing in a place like this? **Anonymous**

Nice place! Do you come here often? **Rupert**

Have my baby, be my baby, what's up baby? **Bebi**

I suppose sex is out of the question? **Heard**

Would you like to fuck me silly? **Anonymous**

I have something in my trousers which I have been saving for you. **Anonymous**

Would you like to suck me to sleep? **Heard**

Where have you been all my life? **Anonymous**

Don't break my heart by telling me you have a boyfriend? **Anonymous**

I want to suck your ... **Heard**

Are they real? This is not a chat up line but... **FI**

Is that a weave? Is that your real hair. I just love women with their own hair, don't you? **Anonymous**

Do you want a shag? (The guy was English, but it worked) **Heard**

Do you lie on your stomach? If she says no, you then say, 'well can I?' **Anonymous**

What are we having for breakfast tomorrow? **Anonymous**

My friend told me a chat-up line I thought could not fail. I was young at the time and did not know any better. The line was this. You go up to a girl you like and ask, 'is your dad a thief?' Obviously she would say no. Then you say, 'who stole the stars for your eyes then?' I had it. I was ready.

I said the line to the first girl I came to (remember I was very young then). To my horror she said her dad was dead. The second time I tried it the girl said yes, 'he is in prison'. I have never used it since. **David**

I want to go to bed with you now. We can use the bathroom. I have protection. Guess what? It did not work. **Anonymous**

27 How do you communicate to your partner that you love her?

NOT for the first time in this book I have discovered what men are suppose to do is not what they actually do. Many men expressed surprise that this question was asked. They thought the answer was obvious. If you love someone you communicate this through words.

Men are seen as callous animals who do not express their love to their partners. I believe this is a myth, just like the one that says men do not cry. I have given up counting the number of men I have seen cry. I doubt very much there is a man out there who can say he has never cried or knows a man who has never cried. Men probably do not cry as much or as easily as women, but they do cry. It is the same with expressing love. We may not say 'I love you' to women as much as women say it to men, but we still say it. **Selestine**

A minority of men said they express love to their partners in different ways–for example when making love or in the things they do for their partners. Men who express their love for their partners in this way often made the comment that their partner sometimes did not think they loved them. The men often retorted. ' If I did not love you I would not have done this or that for you.' Or, 'if I did not love you I would not still be with you'. It is love by action: love communicated not through words but through deed.

When I make love to my woman it is not always for physical gratification. It is one way in which I express my love for her. **Anonymous**

Sometimes when I am really down, either because I had a bad day at work, or because of some other frustration, the only way I feel comfortable and at ease is to be inside my partner. I feel totally at ease and in love with my partner when I am making love to her. **BU**

Some black men are not exposed to men who openly express their feelings when they are growing up. As adults we find it very difficult to tell our women or family we love them. For me the only way to overcome this is to make love to my partner. It is debatable whether women realise that men express love in this way. I have never told my partner of more than 10 years that this is the way I express love to her. **Martin**

I once drove all the way to Southampton (from London) to pick up my girlfriend. To me that is a way of expressing my love for her. **Anonymous**

At Christmas, birthdays or anniversaries I always make sure I buy my partner expensive gifts. **Anonymous**

I have been with my wife for 15 years, for nine of which we lived together as boyfriend and girlfriend. If I did not care about her I would not still be with her or would not have married her. I chose to marry her. I was not forced to. She must know that I love her. I tell all our friends that I love her. I am sure they must have mentioned it to her. **Anonymous**

I took my girlfriend out for a very expensive meal and had a bunch of flowers delivered to our table. I often express love to her in that way. You know, taking her out, being romantic and shit. **Anonymous**

On my girlfriend's 28th birthday I bought her 28 red roses. That was one way I can remember I expressed love to her. **Anonymous**

On my wife's birthday, I brought her breakfast in bed. Afterwards I took her to Paris where we had a fabulous time. **JT**

I brought my partner Champagne in bed for breakfast. We stayed in bed all morning, sipping champagne and making love. That was a very romantic moment I had the pleasure of sharing with my partner. That is some of the crazy shit you do because you love your partner. I do not feel the need to tell her. I prefer to show her. **Jules**

I wrote a poem telling her how much I appreciated her. I had the poem laminated and framed. I posted it to her on the second anniversary of the date we met. **Anonymous**

28 When a man loves a woman

IN the battle that sometimes rages between black men and black women it is all too easy to forget that we do, and can, get together. In the following pages black men talk openly and without reservation about being in love and the way in which they met their partners and the impact finding that special person had on them.

I met my wife through a friend. I was single at the time; the last thing on my mind was meeting someone. My friend told me she knew someone 'just like me' and she thought this stranger and myself would be perfect together. I took great exception to what my friend said. I was single through choice: I never felt I could not get a date if I wanted one. My ego would not let me meet someone through a third party. So I told my friend, thanks but no thanks.

What my friend did was arrange a blind date of sorts. She arranged for a group of us to go to the cinema. We always went out as a group so

I found nothing strange in that. When I got to the cinema there were only three people; my friend, her boyfriend and this other woman. I knew I had been set up. I decided to be miserable and paid little if any attention to my 'blind date'. I hardly spoke to her. The next day my friend called and apologised for trying to fix me up. I accepted the apology and quickly changed the subject.

A week or so later, my friend called and said this same woman wanted to meet me again. I agreed to meet her friend mainly because I wanted to apologise for my behaviour and to tell her the way I acted was nothing personal, I was just not into blind dates.

We met-in of all places-a club. Her sister was doing a PA, so we all went to support her. I do not know what it was, but we were dancing to the Isleys Brothers song 'For the Love of You' and I fell for her. I knew I wanted to see her again.

We built a solid relationship over the next three years. It was not all plain sailing. I must admit at times we came close to breaking up. However, I knew I was really in love with her when she went away for a week and I could not bear to be without her. It was the most horrendous week of my life. When she got back I asked her to marry me. At the wedding the bride requested a song. We danced to the Isleys Brothers 'For the Love of You'. **Andre**

I was ready. I had seen it all and virtually done it all. I was a player before men knew how to be players. I was a player before women knew what a player was. Love never meant a thing to me. When I was growing up no one said they loved me so I never told anyone when I became a man that I loved them. So many women told me they loved me that I thought love was my middle name. In fact, what I did was to call my penis Dr.Love. I knew so many women. It was all a game to me. I never trusted women, especially the ones that said they loved me. I thought they loved Dr.Love and not me.

I knew women who had been going out with their partners for years, women who were married, women who you would think would never give it up unless they were married, women who were engaged, women who swore they would never betray their boyfriends or their best friends. All these women, without exception, fell for me. Looking back I can see now I was lonely and looking for something.

Like I said, I was ready, for what I was not quite sure. I knew I was not happy. I knew I needed more. I knew I was tired of this existence. It was at that time I met Monica. Monica was ordinary. She had this unshakable belief in herself, she was intelligent but humble. She was tall, with brown skin, great legs, natural hair and a smile bestowed upon her face from heaven. She was also a conscious sister who was proud of her blackness and her roots.

I met her at a wedding of a friend; she was there with a guy I knew in passing. I was introduced to her and spent a great deal of time talking to her. I asked her for her telephone number. She refused. I tried all the stuff that I knew had worked on other women. Still she refused. I eventually got her number from the guy she came with. I introduced him to a girl that I knew and in return he gave me her number. The guy, it turned out, only went with her because Monica's friend was sick and the three of them had originally planned to go to the wedding.

The first time I called her she put the phone down on me. I tried again, she said I had no right to call her since she had not given me her number. I apologised and she hung up. That was that for about two or three weeks.

I met Monica again at a conscious event. She was one of the people reading poetry. Afterwards I spoke to her. Without bull, just straight talk. We arranged to meet the following day. On our first meeting she asked why I treated women the way I did. I felt uncomfortable, I tried bluffing my way through, but she saw right through me. So I was honest with her. I told her I was no good and that she should not be with me because I am not capable of loving her or anyone else. I remember I told her I would break her heart just as I have broken many others. To my amazement she looked at me gave me one of her heavenly smiles and said, 'you will love me'. I laughed. I thought she must be crazy after all, we hardly knew each other and here she was talking about love.

Monica and I dated after that night. I found it very difficult giving up my former life although I wanted to. I was honest with Monica and told her I needed time. I wanted to make a commitment to her, but part of me was afraid of loosing the lover boy image.

Monica scared me. So I tried not seeing her for a while. In that time she never called me. But the strange thing was that during that time I never went out with anyone else.

I knew I'd fallen in love with Monica when I woke up one morning after not seeing her for weeks and couldn't remember how I'd coped before she came into my life. I arranged to meet her, and for the first time in my life told her I loved her and wanted to be with her. All she did was looked at me smile and said, 'I told you, you would love me'.

Wayne

I met my partner a very long time ago. At the time we were working for the same company. We were the only black people in an office of 200 plus. I believe that if there had been more black people in the company we would never have got together.

At first I could not stand her. I thought she was a coconut and avoided her like the plague. Whenever I saw her she was with white men, or going to the pub or going all sorts of ridiculous places with white people. My views about her changed when we both went to the pub to celebrate our colleague's birthday. At the pub I thought all my suspicions were confirmed when I heard the conversations she was having with the rest of the office staff. Coconut through and through, I thought.

Later that night we got talking one on one. She asked me why I had not spoken to her, particularly as there were only two of us in the entire company.

'Oh shit', I thought to myself. She wants me to say something and then she will run back to them and say how racist I was and that I should be fired.

'We are on a different floor, I hardly get the chance to see you." I said

'Bullshit,' she shouted.

'I bet you are a typical black man. Once you see a black woman with white company you assume she is a sell-out. You should get to know me before you jump to conclusions,' she said.

She then got up and left. I felt the least I could do was get to know her, see who she was, where she was coming from.

In time I got to know her. She was not a coconut. She was doing what millions of black people do in order to achieve success in a white society. When she was with white people she acted a certain way. We all do it. Some black people go all the way and sell out. The majority of us compromise and do what needs to be done.

I was in line for promotion. I was certain I would get it. She called me congratulating me before the results had come out. However, when the result came out I had been bypassed. The promotion was given to a white boy straight out of university. They said I did not have the qualifications, so they gave it to somebody who I trained.

I had planned to meet Debbie in the canteen because I knew it would be empty by the time I got the news. Well we met. When she saw me she held me for what seem an eternity. In that time I forgot all my troubles. Not a word was spoken. We just hugged. She must have heard the bad news.

This may sound corny, but Debbie took away all the hurt, anger and frustration I felt after hearing that I had been passed over for promotion yet again. At that precise time, and at that precise moment in the canteen was when I decided I wanted this beautiful black woman in my life permanently. We have been together now for over ten years. We have two children and a third on the way. **Robert**

It was just like the records said it would be. I had found my soul mate. I felt as if Teddy Pendergrass, Marvin Gaye and Barry White were all singing about me. I could not have expressed it any better. I was in love. The world was a great, joyous and wonderful place. That feeling in my stomach lasted for a year or more. Then it all started to go wrong. The more I saw of Virginia, the more I thought I had made a mistake. We argued all the time. We hardly went out. There never seemed to be any money although we were both working.

Maybe I am too young to settle down. Teddy Pendergrass was wrong. Barry White could not have been here, not with this woman. Luther Vandross must have been crazy singing about, 'A House Is not a home'. These were the thoughts going through my mind on a daily basis. I felt trapped. A day did not go by when I did not pick an argument or give Virginia a reason to leave me. Virginia to her credit, hung on in there. She obviously saw something I did not. She never gave up on me or the relationship. She just gave me space to figure out the shit I was going through.

What I originally felt with Virginia was good. We were in love with each other and with life. No one existed but us. After a while things changed; to make matters worst she got pregnant. Like a lot of men, when the going got tough I got up and left. I did not want to have a child. At my insistence she had an abortion. I went to pick her up at the hospital. I had only agreed to pick her up because I thought it was the least I could do.

I next saw Virginia in hospital a few weeks later. Complications had arisen connected to the abortion. Something in me changed when I saw her. I realised for the first time I was a coward and a fool for walking out. I cried when I saw her. I felt ashamed for not being a man and taking responsibility for my actions. The grass is not greener on the other side. The grass is as green on your side. A relationship takes work. To love and care for someone is a serious business. It may not be for everyone.

I love Virginia. I feel blessed that she took me back after all my madness. Every day that I wake up and she is there next to me I thank the Lord. We have been together almost seven years. Through thick and thin we have remained with each other. **Leon**

The first and only time I believe I was in love was with a girl called Louise. It was at school. We were both in our final year. She was short, very dark with a beautiful body and a great smile. At first I thought it was lust. I thought about her all the time, the size of her breasts, her short legs, her full lips. I really looked forward to seeing her.

She was new to the school. She had recently arrived from the West Indies. I loved the way she spoke, although some of the guys made fun of her accent. On a school outing we began to talk. I more or less told her how I felt. She was surprised. I believe she had never noticed me before, certainly not in a romantic way. Eventually we started to date. We dated secretly because she told me her parents did not want her to see any boy particularly when exams were only a year away.

We saw each other every day after school. When we were meant to be in the library studying for exams we were either in a cinema or walking in the park or doing something we should not have been doing. She was the first person I made love to.

We both failed our exams. Her parents were so angry that they sent her back home. I have never seen her since. That was about 17 years ago. I have never forgotten her. I have cared for other women, but I have never experienced what I did with Louise. She was special. She was unique. At times I still miss her. Someone once said to me, 'Count yourself lucky if you find love once in your life'. I guest I am lucky to have loved one woman. **Bernie**

I had a serious reputation for being a sexist. The first two years I lived with my girlfriend I never cooked or did any housework. I always wanted a woman who was not afraid of the kitchen, and housework in particular. My girlfriend's family and friends told her she should leave me.

My girlfriend was confined to bed for months on end after a hysterectomy. We did not have any children. Her friends predicted that I would leave her within two months. I did not leave. What I did was to change my attitude. I learned to cook, I made sure she did not do any housework. I gave her flowers every week and brought her breakfast in bed. I know I am now trying. My only regret was that it took a horrendous incident for me to see what was so clear to everyone else.

My girlfriend is now up and about. I still cook and share the household chores. Everyday I am with her I try to make up for my sexist attitude. That is what love does to you. **Gerry**

I was lonely. My last serious relationship was two years ago. I have had brief encounters with women during the last two years-nothing serious though. I was old, too old I felt, for going to clubs every weekend. I definitely did not want to listen to jungle or the latest craze in music. I thought the music was for younger younger people. At 29 I did not feel young. Approaching 30, I wanted more than hanging out at clubs. The women I seem to attract wanted to go to clubs every weekend. I thought the raving scene was getting younger. It was not. I was getting older.

I remembered when I first started going to clubs I used to watch the older people and wondered what they were doing here with so many young people. I thought they should be anywhere but here. I saw that same look in the faces of the young people in the clubs. I felt it was time to retire from the club scene. We all reach that point. For me it was at 29. For others it is 49 or 69.

According to magazines, black women should be all over me. I am employed, educated, own a two bedroom house. I drive a reasonable car and earn a reasonable salary. I believe I have average features, and a good solid body. I must be doing something wrong because there were no damn women.

I turned 30 on June 29. I felt like shit. No woman in over two years, serious one that is. New decade same old life. I felt so low that I thought of calling my ex to see if she would take pity on me and offer me a sympathy fuck. In the end I decided against it.

For my birthday I arranged to meet some friends at a very nice black-owned restaurant in North London. It was more their idea than mine. David, a close friend of mine, came into the restaurant with a woman I knew I had to have. Yes, I thought to myself, this is my wife and on my birthday too! David was a player. He always had a new woman. This one, however, was different from his usual type. For one thing she was classy. For another she could actually hold a knife and fork and speak the Queen's English.

David is from the old school. He and I go way back. We used to run a sound system back in the days. He watched my back. I also had his back covered. David came up to me on my birthday and said the woman he came in with was for me. She was my type and therefore was my birthday gift. Shit, David was my boy! I was not about to tell him he was sexist and he should not treat women that way. Besides, I wanted this woman. She was going to be my wife. I found love on my birthday.

After that night at the restaurant I got to know Janice. She was all that I wanted. She, however, was not ready to settle down. I wanted to get married, have kids and discover new pastures. She wanted to be free, go to fucking clubs and develop her career. Maybe in three years she said she might be ready to settle down. Shit! I could not wait. In three years I would be almost 34. She would be 28. After seeing each other for ten months we agreed to split.

The best thing to come out of the relationship was that Janice made me realise I was getting old, but I was no way as old as I made out. She also made me realise I was too desperate to have kids and settle down. I should take my time and not rush, because by rushing I am more than likely to make the wrong choice.

She was right. I changed my attitude. I still wanted to get married but I was no longer in a hurry. I disagreed with her on certain points. There was definitely no way I was going back to the club scene on a regular basis. Neither would I go out with a woman who still wanted to go to clubs on a regular basis. I was not willing to compromise on that point.

Twenty two months later, at the age of 33 plus, I am a very proud father of a very big baby girl. She was almost nine pounds at birth. Her mother's name is Sharon. She is only a year younger than me. She hates going to clubs. She is a born again Christian. I am not religious, but we have compromised on certain issues. She will not try to convert me to her religion and I will respect her right to follow what ever religion she chooses.

I have never felt like this before about anyone. In the past I thought I was in love, but I was wrong. Betty Shabazz, the wife of the late Malcolm X, said on the Oprah Winfrey show, 'It is best to find a man when he is ready'. She said she found Malcolm when he was ready. He had done and experienced so many things that he was ready to settle down when they met.

At the time I did not know, appreciate or fully understand what Betty Shabazz meant. I am not in the slightest way comparing myself to Malcolm X. But I do know now what she meant. It is best to get a man when he is ready. Two years ago I was not ready I thought I was and made the right noise, but deep down I was not ready. Today I am ready.

I met Sharon in a well-known fast food restaurant. It was not love at first sight, it was more physical attraction at first sight. She had the biggest tits that ever squeezed into a small top. I approached her and gave her my number. She called me about a week or so later. We talked for days before she agreed to meet me. The rest is history.

You should never ever give up on love. You will find it. I found what I wanted at the age of 33. You never know when Cupid is going to strike. **Rudi**

29 Last words

I end this book with a poem written by one of the men I interviewed. He wrote the poem for his 'black queen'. Before they met she was involved in a very abusive relationship which resulted in her withdrawing from black men. He does not know whether she loves him or trusts him. Nevertheless, he wanted to dedicate the poem to his black queen in order to prove his love for her and his dedication to her. He also wanted to dedicate the poem to black men and women who are searching for that special someone or to those who have found that special person.

When a man loves a woman
He will do her no wrong
When a man loves a woman
He will love her strong
When a man loves a woman
He will not abuse

Her mind, body or soul
As he knows that is
Not the way true love goes

When a man loves a woman
She will not be lonely
When a man loves a woman
He will love her unconditionally
When a man loves a woman
He will come home to her
As he knows no other

When a man loves a woman
He will understand her pain
As it is his pain too
When a man loves a woman
He will understand her struggle
As it is his struggle too
When a man loves a woman
They will become strong as they become one

When a black man loves a black woman...

THE END?

ORDER FORM

FROM THE
Mouths of Men

'From the Mouths of Men' is available through mail order.

Further copies can be ordered directly from the publisher by filling in this form (photocopies are acceptable).

Please send me ______ copies of ***'From the Mouths of Men'*** at £5.99 each (includes postage and packing - UK only).

Please enclosed a cheque or postal order made payable to: Inglis Publications, and send to, Inglis Publications, PO Box 16819, London E13 9RP.

TITLE FIRST NAME FAMILY NAME

ADDRESS

POST CODE

You may receive further information or offers from Inglis Publications or other carefully selected third parties which may be of interest to you. If you do not wish to receive such offers, please tick this box ☐

Alwin Peter is now preparing a new book on love, romance and sex. He would like to hear from you with your stories about finding love, keeping love and lost love. Also, have you ever taken revenge on a partner who cheated on you? If yes, what did you do?

ROMANCE: Have you done anything you considered romantic?

SEX: What are your sexual fantasies?

Please send your stories, suggestions or comments to:
Alwin Peter
c/o Inglis Publications
PO Box 16819
London
E13 9RP

All information will be treated in confidence.
Personal details will not be published.